Refining Moments

Refining Moments: Shaping Your Successes and Setbacks into Significance
Copyright© 2014 Gregory K. Hernandez

All rights reserved. No part of this book may be reproduced in any form or by any mechanical means, including information storage and retrieval systems without permission in writing from the publisher/author, except by a reviewer, who may quote passages in a review. Scanning, uploading, and electronic distribution of this book or the facilitation of such without the permission of the publisher/author is prohibited. Please support the author's rights by purchasing only authorized electronic editions, and not participating in electronic piracy of copyrighted materials. Any member of educational institutions wishing to photocopy part or all of the work for classroom use, or anthology, should send inquiries to gkh@gkarlco.com.

Library of Congress Control Number: 2014911260

ISBN: 978-0-9905174-0-5

1. SELF-HELP / Personal Growth / Success
2. BUSINESS & ECONOMICS / Personal Finance / Retirement Planning
3. BUSINESS & ECONOMICS / Personal Success

QUANTITY PURCHASES: Companies, professional groups, clubs, and other organizations may qualify for special terms when ordering quantities of this title. For information e-mail gkh@gkarlco.com.

This book is printed in the United States of America.

Refining Moments

Shaping Your Successes and Setbacks into Significance

Gregory K. Hernandez

This book is dedicated to
my wife and best friend for life, Rebecca;
our sons Michael, Nicholas, and Jonathan,
and their families; and our parents
Greg, Ruth, Jim, and Freda.
Your love and support
are a gift from God.

CONTENTS

Acknowledgments 11
Foreword 13
Introduction 19

SECTION I: REFINING MOMENTS DISCOVERED 27
    Chapter 1: My Start in Life 29
    Chapter 2: Refining Moments Defined 37
    Chapter 3: The Million-Dollar Taco 43
    Chapter 4: Road to Professional Development 47
    Chapter 5: Welcome to Corporate America 53

SECTION II: EMOTIONAL REFINEMENT 65
    Chapter 6: The Benefits of a Learning
        vs. a Performance Orientation 67
    Chapter 7: Pride 83
    Chapter 8: Anger 91
    Chapter 9: Attitude 95
    Chapter 10: Spirituality 99
    Chapter 11: Meaningful Conversations 105

SECTION III: PHYSICAL REFINEMENT 113
    Chapter 12: "It's Opening Night" 115
    Chapter 13: Routine Medical Examinations 123
    Chapter 14: Nutrition 127

Chapter 15: Exercise	133
Chapter 16: Rest and Recovery	139

SECTION IV: FINANCIAL REFINEMENT   145
     Chapter 17: Where Are We?
         Where Are We Going?   147
     Chapter 18: Financial Planning Fundamentals   157

SECTION V: PROFILES OF REFINEMENT   173
     Chapter 19: A New Millennium:
         Violet Igolnikov   175
     Chapter 20: Bank Teller to CEO:
         "Mr. Wilson"   183
     hapter 21: Season of Transition   189
     Chapter 22: Rags to Riches to Contentment:
         Daniel Decker   193
     Chapter 23: Closing Thoughts   205

SECTION VI: REFINEMENT VS. RETIREMENT   209
     Chapter 24: What Do I Want to
         Be When I Grow Up?   211
     Chapter 25: Where Do We Go from Here?   217

Meet the Author   225

ACKNOWLEDGMENTS

THIS BOOK IS WRITTEN WITH gratitude to my immediate and extended family for shaping my life. Our grandparents provided us with a legacy of significance.

A special thanks to friends and business associates throughout the years for mentoring me far beyond what anyone might have expected.

Thank you to the ministries of High Desert Church, Bayside Granite Bay, and Plum Creek Community for refining my life over the past 20 years.

A special shout-out to Steve, the baristas, and patrons at Espressolé Caffe for providing a creative environment for writing.

Thank you to the team at Polly Letofsky, My Word! Publishing. Your patience and persistence brought this book to fruition.

And finally, a special thank you to my editor, Susan Hindman, for understanding and clarifying my voice.

FOREWORD

"OH HOW I KNOW THE joys of sitting in a 50th floor executive office with a view of the Hollywood Hills sign, wearing the finest of suits and driving the finest of cars. I also know the helpless feeling of packing up your personal belongings and taking them down that 50th floor elevator to the ground floor."

These are some of the important words coming from Gregory Hernandez's book, *Refining Moments*.

My father always told me as a young boy to never trust anyone who says, "Trust me." "Trust is never asked for, it is given to only those deserving," he would say to me over and over.

Many of you picking up this book may not know or trust Gregory Hernandez, but I do. And he is a very special man. And, in my opinion, anyone with the guts to write those words above obviously has something important to teach us all. Gregory has learned one of life's greatest lessons: humility. And I choose to listen to a man who knows what it is like taking the elevator DOWN from the 50th floor.

One of my favorite movies is *My Life*, a 1993 American film starring Michael Keaton and Nicole Kidman. In 1993 I was a year out of college finding my way and stumbling through my first job. But that movie struck a genuine chord with me. In short, Bob Jones (played by Keaton) is having his first child with his wife, Gail, played by Kidman. Shortly after the news that they are having a baby boy, Bob learns that he has been diagnosed with a terminal illness (kidney cancer). Wanting his son to know who he is and to share important fatherly lessons, he decides to make a video for his unborn child. Bob teaches him how to shave, play basketball, cook spaghetti, and even how to start a car by jumper cable.

If roles were reversed and I learned that I was dying, I would make a much different video. I'd want to teach my kids about love, faith, relationships, pride, power of positive attitude, gratitude, humility, how to have meaningful conversations, nutrition, investing, and financial management.

What if I told you all these topics would be addressed by Gregory in his new book? And what if I told you they are addressed in a meaningful, humble, and caring way?

Would you commit to not only reading this important book, but passing it on to your kids and friends?

A few years ago, before we moved north, my wife and I attended Plum Creek Community Church in Castle Rock, Colorado. It was there I joined my first men's group Bible study. I was not looking forward to sitting in a circle of men telling me how perfect their lives are. Perfect job. Perfect marriage. Perfect kids. You know the drill.

And then I met Gregory Hernandez, the guy sitting next to me at Bible study. Man, was I wrong.

You are going to like this book, but more importantly, love Gregory's heart for teaching and serving others.

Tommy Spaulding
Author of the *New York Times* best seller
It's Not Just Who You Know

RE·FINE
verb \ri-'fīn\
: to remove the unwanted substances in (something)
: to improve (something) by making small changes

RE·FINE·MENT
noun \ri-'fīn-ment\
: the act or process of removing unwanted substances from something: the act or process of making something pure
: the act or process of improving something
: an improved version of something
(www.merriam-webster.com)

: the process of removing impurities or unwanted elements from a substance; the improvement or clarification of something by the making of small changes."
(Oxford dictionaires.com | Oxford University Press)

REFINING MOMENT
A moment that places you on your path, purpose, or calling in life

INTRODUCTION

IS THERE ROOM FOR ANOTHER book about success? If it radically changes what we think of as success and how we achieve it, then I believe yes.

We have been taught from an early age that if you go off to college, marry, work hard, and invest wisely, you can retire to a life of leisure at the perfect age of 65. For many years, this has been defined as the American dream and success.

And judging by our Facebook postings, daily tweets, beautiful homes and cars, and numerous technological gadgets, we must be doing great.

But really, how's that working out for you?

The truth is, maybe it is time to adjust our definition of success and redefine our expectations about retirement.

Have you met college graduates working in jobs far below their educational expectations? Will they ever be on track to buy a home, let alone save for the future? Fortunately, they have many years to get this *right*, not just figure it out. This book can help.

How about the middle-age and boomer populations? With far fewer years to invest, how many will be able to rely on a pension like their parents? A growing number of discouraged people already know the answer to this.

A new definition of success needs to be declared, with a new pathway forged. The new success will require a desire to live a life of passion, purpose, and significance in spite of your savings account. And the new success will require a willingness to *refine* your daily activities in three dynamic areas of life: your emotional-spiritual-relational health, your physical health, and your financial health. Think of *refining* as making small changes that create lifelong improvement. I also refer to *refining moments*, which are critical events—large or small, good or bad—that occur and have the power to change you for the better. I will present examples throughout the book that will bring about a better understanding of all of this.

Retirement is not a goal or a destination. Truly understanding this will release you from the pressure of trying to figure out how to attain it. Rather than retirement, embrace a life of refinement. Noticing those moments of refinement leads to life lessons that have the ability to launch you into a phenomenal, extraordinary second half of life.

At the time of this writing, our country has been experiencing a challenging economic environment of historic proportions, filled with unemployment, foreclosures, an uncertain stock market, a credit crisis, the closure of hundreds of small businesses, and large corporations searching for the next merger in order to survive. It should be no surprise that consumer sentiment—how we feel about our immediate economic future—has been at an all-time low.

Unfortunately, like our economic environment, our political environment is no better off. It does not matter which side of the political spectrum you call home: most likely, you are deeply disappointed. It is easy to point fingers at our economy and our politicians. The purpose of this book is to help us take control of what we can control: ourselves. We all naturally excel in some area(s) of our lives and ignore others vital to our total well-being. We ignore that our own shortcomings can cause us to face our career and personal relationships like plastic-action-figure politicians. We present ourselves to the public—or worse, to our families—with a politician's smile. We fail to admit that we do not have all the answers, and we are fearful of seeking out the resources that can actually help us. We unintentionally hold ourselves back from reaching our full potential.

Think of the resume heading, "I am uniquely qualified for (fill in the blank)." What have your life lessons and experiences uniquely qualified you for? Review your life's journey. It will assist you in discovering your path, purpose, and calling in life, whether you're 30 or 65.

I contemplated writing *Refining Moments* for a number of years. But I was waiting until I had everything together: perfect health, perfect happiness, and perfect wealth.

Warning: I do not have it all together. Yet I hope that helps to bring even more authenticity to the table. In Section I, I will share some stories from my life's journey that throughout my corporate career were too embarrassing to acknowledge. As I am now in the second half of life and approaching the age of retirement, I am forced to take an honest look in the mirror and learn from my past to help create my future. In doing so, I hope to help you discover your story and your lessons learned.

Oh how I know the joys of sitting in a 50th-floor executive office with a view of the Hollywood Hills sign, wearing the finest of suits and driving the finest of cars. I also know the helpless feeling of packing up your personal belongings and taking them down that 50th-floor elevator to the ground floor.

This happened three times. I received three "financial packages" from the same firm. The first package was all-inclusive: psychological and career counseling, a prestigious office with a receptionist to give the impression you are still employed, and a professional support system. The last package gave me only a simpler office on the other side of the city. I will never forget what must have appeared to be a pitiful group of has-beens—former co-workers, now unemployed, drinking punch in a beat-up conference room, doing their best to spread some holiday cheer.

I know what it is like to travel to some of the finest destinations the world has to offer, eat at the finest restaurants, drink the finest wines, and walk into a room with your head held up high. Likewise, I know what it is like to pay for your groceries with food stamps and do your best to ignore the stares of the curious with your head held low.

I know what it is like for your family to be viewed as a picture of perfection. And I know the pain of separating from that picture-perfect family for a period of time while my wife and I worked out our issues.

I know what it is like to run a race, to feel the oxygen flowing freely in and out of your lungs, and to raise your arms in victory as you cross the finish line. And I know what it is like to go back to your big-boy suit after ignoring your doctor's warning to shed a few pounds or else.

This book is a call to action in your three dynamic areas of life, mentioned above: your emotional-spiritual-relational health (explored more deeply in Section II), your physical health (in Section III), and your financial health (in Section IV).

No one has it all together. But the joy in life is finding your life's purpose and doing your very best to meet the challenges associated with living out that purpose. There is always more distance to travel. There is no such thing as "I have arrived" or "My work is complete and I am retired." As far as I am concerned, the word *retirement* should be removed from the English dictionary. As long as I am alive, I am going to live a life of refinement, a life of continuous improvement.

Success is not where you are but the distance traveled from where you started.

SECTION I

REFINING MOMENTS DISCOVERED

CHAPTER 1

MY START IN LIFE

I AM A HISPANIC MALE, born to Ruth and Greg Hernandez. I have a younger brother and a younger sister. We were not Catholic, I did not speak Spanish, and the majority of my grammar-school friends and their parents had blond hair and blue eyes. Welcome to my childhood in Los Angeles, circa 1964. My mom lovingly recalls the time I came home from school and asked her to dye her hair blond and add the cute little flip like all the TV moms.

She was born in Ventura, California, in the 1930s and raised in East Los Angeles, already a diverse melting pot. She appreciated the different backgrounds represented in her neighborhood: Mexican-American, African-American, Japanese, Chinese, Christian, and Jewish. Mom often shared stories of her adventurous childhood and growing-up years. Always the class clown, she enjoyed the limelight and loved to perform in her high school's stage productions; she was blessed with a beautiful soprano voice.

My father was born in San Antonio, Texas, the son of hardworking parents who often moved to where work in the fields could be secured. My dad spent much of his childhood living on a farm in Port Huron, Michigan, and he was forced to drop out of school in the eighth grade to assist his family with additional income. At 16 he jumped on a Greyhound bus and traveled by himself to Los Angeles in search of a way to support his parents and siblings. Naturally shy, Dad has a work ethic like none other, and once you get to know him, you discover a surprising sense of humor that can reduce you to tears.

My parents bought their first home in what was considered the suburbs at the time, approximately 20 miles outside of Los Angeles. Their desire was to raise a family away from the changing influences of the big city. They had witnessed both sides of the success equation: those who had succumbed to the pressures of gangs, alcoholism, and poverty; and those who had strived to provide a better life with all the opportunities they had been given. My parents felt they had a God-given responsibility to take what had been entrusted to them from their parents and bring it up a notch or two for their children. My mom would often sing, "Some are lucky and some are not, so just be grateful, for what you've got"—to which my sister, Lucy, once sarcastically replied at a very young age, "Yeah ... and we have to be grateful!"

As children, at school and in our neighborhood, I was like most others. I strived to fit in and learned to adapt because we all have a need to seek acceptance. Since grade school, I have developed my powers of observation, and this became a management and leadership skill that I continued to develop. Always feeling just a bit different from the others, I learned how to quickly assess the environment or any given situation.

> **"Yeah ... and we have to be grateful!"**

Perhaps more so than other students, I was determined to not only fit in with a group but also seek a way to add value. Is there something I can contribute to the conversation? Is there something positive or encouraging that I can offer?

I attended Rowland High School, a fairly large school, and finished around 254th in my class. My ranking is consistent with much of my high school life. I hung out with some of the popular kids as well as with the less-popular, somewhat nerdy kids. I played trumpet in the marching band during freshman year. I discovered I loved running (and the associated weight loss), and I joined the cross-country and track teams, lettering in my junior year. I also played guitar and could appear to be cool playing it on the school lawn. And I could impressively play Elton John's "Your Song" on an available piano. (People were often surprised at how well I could play, not knowing I had studied piano from the ages of 5 to 17.) I was not a hunk by any means, but I was good-looking enough that I far surpassed my social expectations.

My childhood and teenage years provided me with a communication and relational skill set that served, and continues to serve, me well. Like my father, I developed a sense of humor; like my mother, I enjoyed performing along with any opportunity to be onstage. I was always considered somewhat mature for my age, and I'll never forget when an influential adult in my life said that I had "a natural sense of charisma."

In high school, I was enrolled in the various college preparatory courses, and my parents' desire was for me to do well in school. But there were many times my homework was not being monitored, and I was prone to slacking off. In my first semester of geometry, I was assigned to the front row. There I completed all of my homework assignments and received an A. The second semester, I had made new friends, sat in the back row, and my grade deteriorated to an F. My parents and I had no idea what an SAT examination entailed, so I had absolutely no preparation. I just knew you were supposed to take this test if you wanted to attend college. I was in for an educational beating. (Thank God for community college!)

I met my future wife, Becky, in the eighth grade, through a local church youth group. She went on to attend Walnut High School, on the better side of the tracks.

We were at the opposite ends of the middle-class spectrum. Her father, Jim, was an accountant and financial officer, and my father was employed in retail sales at Sears and Roebuck (actually, my father always worked two jobs). The great thing about our relationship is she and I were friends, and we socialized and traveled in groups of friends. By senior year, we were planning our wedding.

Becky finished high school midyear with honors, top of her class, and she was now engaged to this likable Hispanic kid with a C, maybe C+ grade-point average? We were both already enrolled and taking extra classes in a local community college; but, admittedly, our financial prospects were bleak. However, we knew beyond a shadow of a doubt that somehow we were going to make it.

Our wedding was attended by at least 100 family members and friends, and at the conclusion of our finger-sandwich reception in the church social hall, we headed off in our pea-green Ford Pinto to our honeymoon destination: Disneyland, approximately 25 miles away. I wonder how many people thought we would have any chance of survival.

A moment in time, that may seem significant or not, inspirational, detrimental, or non-monumental; a moment that when recognized, created, or embraced can place you on your path, purpose, or calling in life; and for this reason, this moment will forever be known as a refining moment

CHAPTER 2

REFINING MOMENTS DEFINED

SO WHAT HAPPENED NEXT? MANY jobs and pay scales, the birth of a family, financial vulnerability, good planning, and lack of planning.

What I learned is that life always presents us with what I call refining moments—moments that will make or break us, shape us, and, if we allow, refine us. These moments can take a life that might appear to be nothing more than a lump of ore and transform it into a priceless piece of precious metal. And truthfully, there may come a time when we need to melt down the precious metal by taking a few steps back and starting over again. These moments can enrich our lives, refining us toward a greater purpose—a life purpose.

These moments can enrich our lives, refining us toward a greater purpose—a life purpose.

Refining moments come about in our daily thoughts, actions, and interactions. Most may seem insignificant at the moment they occur. Think of a time when you realized that a "chance meeting" or flippant response to a situation had a profound impact, for better or for worse, in ways that you would have never imagined. It is my belief and my experience that by learning to recognize and cultivate our refining moments, we can lead a life of greater significance and achieve a more balanced definition of success.

Let's talk for a moment about what success looks like. Why is it that most of us measure success in terms of money? Why is it that when meeting someone, the first way in which we tend to define ourselves is in terms of our occupation? Obviously, money and financial security are extremely important. My professional career has revolved around helping others to attain and maintain financial success, which can be defined as the ability to live in a manner in which you are accustomed, whether or not you choose to work.

But the majority of us are failing miserably in that regard. Various studies and surveys show that around 80 percent of the American population is not saving enough to be on course for retiring at the age of 65. The traditional view of success and the ability to retire just won't happen.

How do I view financial success? An example that I have used in my financial presentations is a photograph of a Walmart greeter—a senior citizen wearing a blue vest with a bright yellow smiley face. "Is this an example of success?" I ask the audience. After some discussion, someone will come up with the right answer: "It depends."

The reason it's right is this: Let's imagine this greeter is in good health, enjoys the camaraderie of co-workers, loves the social interaction with the public, and is earning extra cash to fire up the motor home and head off to see the grandkids. That's absolutely success! But what if instead this greeter needs the job in order to put a loaf of bread on the table and is completely exhausted and stressed out? That is probably not the "success" any of us would purposely choose. What about the successful executive or business owner who is at the top of the financial food chain but very much alone or in poor health? Would we choose this for our own success?

Now back to refining moments. I have come to discover three broad categories of refining moments. Daily, ongoing improvement in all three areas is a necessity for living a life that provides a meaningful societal impact and can have a dynamic impact for generations to come. Excelling in all three areas is what I call success.

- **Emotionally refining moments (ERM)**: This category relates to our heart and soul. It includes our relational, spiritual, and mental well-being.

Far more than just maintaining a positive attitude, ERM includes thoughts and actions that nourish us at the very core of who we are and why we are here. ERM includes our internal dialogue or secret conversations we have with ourselves.

- **Physically refining moments (PRM):** Our physical body houses our heart and soul. Our physical well-being is instrumental in determining our capacity to recover from illness and stress. Our level of energy and stamina helps fuel us toward our goals in life. Our outward physical appearance is often a manifestation of our overall general health.
- **Financially refining moments (FRM):** The management of our financial resources and skill sets. Our education and skill set provides us with the ability to work and cover life's basic necessities (planned and unplanned) as well as the ability to assist others. In terms of money, each day we can make more, save more, or both. The accumulation of monetary resources provides us with a freedom of choice. We can choose where as well as how we want to live.

The challenge is to purposefully develop all three refining moments.

While we have a natural tendency to gravitate toward one area or the other, the challenge is to purposefully develop all three refining moments.

Think of a situation where someone tends to focus on only one key area. How about the social butterfly who has the gift of gab and plenty of friends but not enough money or adequate health care to provide for her own basic physical needs. Maybe this social butterfly has been to one too many potluck dinners and may be grossly overweight. Because she lacks the FRM to provide for her PRM, her life could be cut short due to poor health.

Or how about the health club jock who drinks protein shakes, pumps iron, runs, rides, and participates in triathlons but cannot seem to hold down a job. And socially, he moves from one fitness bombshell to the next. While there is no shortage of PRM, he is sorely missing the mark in terms of FRM and ERM.

Of course, we have all witnessed the financial genius. Making lots of money seems to come naturally. He has all the toys the world has to offer and seems to stand so tall even when seated in a luxury car cruising down the highway without a care in the world. Yet, in his quietest hour, deep inside his heart of hearts, he knows … Not a care in the world? Maybe. Except no one cares! If his money vanished, the "friends" and associates he does have would be nowhere to be found. Relationally, he is bankrupt. There is an abundance of FRM at the expense of ERM and more than likely PRM.

It doesn't have to be this way. We all have an amazing capacity to learn, to start over if necessary, and to refine ourselves toward a greater purpose.

Which brings me to my first job: "Yo quiero Taco Bell!"

CHAPTER 3

THE MILLION-DOLLAR TACO

HOW IN THE WORLD CAN you discover a financially refining moment while stirring beans and making tacos at a fast-food restaurant?

This FRM—my first on-the-job career lesson—would prove to be profound enough to change my life. While it was a moment that may not have been fully appreciated at the time, it ultimately placed me on a path toward years of a six-figure income and a lifestyle I would never have imagined.

So here I am, 18 years old, married, a child on the way, and living with my parents. I am employed at the neighborhood Taco Bell, earning less than $2.50 per hour. I wear a hairnet and go home late at night smelling like Mexican fast food (not that there is anything wrong with that...). By now, I had done a pretty good job of developing my emotional skill set; I was quite sociable and had grown accustomed to people commenting about how mature I was. As far as my financial skill set, I guess my only strength at the time was the work ethic that my father had modeled throughout my childhood. I was happy at work and happy to do a good job.

One day, the store manager, Amir, approaches me in front of my co-workers and comments that he could see me quickly progressing to an assistant manager position. Truthfully, I was embarrassed by the attention, so I casually shrugged off his comment.

"Yeah me, an assistant manager," I sarcastically responded.

Amir snapped at me, in front of the other employees. "Step outside!"

I was embarrassed.

The two of us stood in the back parking lot, next to the trash compactor, and Amir proceeded to lay into me. "I see something in you! You could be moving up to a position that would pay you $800 a month. I mention the word *management* and you laugh? How is it that you are going to lead these people when they hear you laughing and joking about your abilities and future?"

> **"I see something in you!"**

And that was my FRM.

Even so, my career at Taco Bell was short-lived. It's not that I didn't appreciate the company or working for Amir. My friends (my ERM network) had directed me to a higher-paying job and a new career path—as a dishwasher! Now this felt like a real job. It was at a hospital, with a Human Resources department, a photo name badge, more hours, and more money. The work was fast-paced—when those food trays came in from the hospital wings, food, suds, and sprayers went flying everywhere.

As an ERM side note, I don't think I've ever worked with a more sincere, caring group of people. After son Gregory Michael was born, I showed up to work one day, and like a scene out of *An Officer and a Gentleman*, the dishwashers, cooks, and dietary staff gave me an ovation and a surprise baby shower, complete with a cake, presents, and a large stuffed animal. It was hard not to burst into tears.

It did not take long for management to come knocking. One afternoon, the food service manager approached me and said that he saw something in me and what would I think about becoming a cold foods worker? I would prepare food items and occasionally deliver them directly to patients on the floor. The change of position did not come with any extra pay, but if this manager saw something in me, I was going for it.

Now I showed up to work dressed in a nicer pair of slacks and a professional white smock, kind of like a food doctor. I enjoyed staying clean—no more mashed potatoes splat on my plastic apron—and from time to time, I had an opportunity to leave the kitchen and wander through the hospital hallways, a totally different environment.

The hallway floors were polished, there was a décor of stainless steel, and the nurses looked so busy and professional. One young man impressed me with his level of coolness and professionalism. He wore a white smock similar to mine, had a stethoscope around his neck, and wheeled some important-looking equipment from room to room. He would confer with the nurses, and then he would sit at the nurses' station and write down notes in the patients' chart.

What would it be like to work in such a professional environment?

What would it be like to help people in their time of need?

What in the world is a respiratory therapist?

CHAPTER 4

ROAD TO PROFESSIONAL DEVELOPMENT

SUNDAY AFTERNOONS AT THE MILLARDS, my in-laws, bring nothing but the fondest of memories. Becky, Michael, and I had a very simple existence in 1977. I worked, came home (still my parents' house), and went to church with them on Sunday. The nursery provided a much-needed relief for Becky. Our parents and siblings attended the same church, as did our friends from our former youth group. The Young Married class, which we were welcomed into, provided a valuable support system; it was truly an ongoing ERM network, including spiritual growth every single weekend.

A church can be a wonderful example of the good, the bad, and the ugly. You have an opportunity to learn from those who are on a good path, as well as those who are pretending to be on a holier-than-thou path.

You have a weekly opportunity to develop many superficial relationships or, if you work at it, some long-lasting, authentic ones. No one has it all together, but we can surround ourselves with people who are attempting to refine their lives.

Our after-church routine was pretty much the same. We would head over to the Millards' house for Sunday lunch. My favorite meal was homemade lasagna or an In-N-Out Burger. Maybe not quite on track with my PRM; but, I later learned, if you are going to have fast food, an In-N-Out burger is healthier than most!

"Gratitude + Expectation = Attitude"

Following lunch, I would resume my weekly search through the classified section of the *Los Angeles Times* in hopes of finding a new career path. This was years before the Internet. It has been said that "Gratitude + Expectation = Attitude," and my attitude was sky-high as I flipped through the pages and clipped employment opportunities. I have always lived with a deep sense of gratitude for the sacrifices of my parents and their parents in seeking a better life. And I have always had a gleeful expectation that there is so much more that can come our way.

In another life-changing FRM, my mother-in-law, Freda, came across an article in the newspaper about a technical school with a respiratory therapy program. The article also announced that there were a limited number of grants available to cover the full cost of tuition. I couldn't believe it! I had already observed respiratory therapists in action!

Looking back, my family—dependent on our parents, food stamps, and family assistance programs—could have imploded at any time. Like most men, I faced a battle with my sense of self-worth, pride, and ego—something I have dealt with all my life. But I am so grateful that through these refining moments, I could swallow my pride. Becky and I continued to live with my parents, and I applied for and was accepted into the respiratory therapy program with full tuition. I studied very hard for one year, with assistance from Becky every single night, and then began a year of employment to become eligible for a national certification exam.

What I learned during those two years, for the first time ever, was that I was smart. People were asking me for help. I passed the national exam on my first attempt. As I would head off to work, I was eager to fully apply myself and be as professional as I could possibly be. I learned my signature, as funny as that may sound, meant something. I would enter notes into patients' medical records and sign my name: Greg K. Hernandez, CRTT (Certified Respiratory Therapy Technician) and later RCP (Respiratory Care Practitioner).

As a member of the Code Blue team, I never knew what I might encounter next, and I learned to appreciate that life is but a vapor that can quickly vanish. I observed people dealing with life and death, fear and triumph, regrets and satisfaction. These refining moments helped me to determine what is really important in life.

My career lasted for eight years at two hospitals. During this time, I supplemented our income with two, sometimes three jobs, at other hospitals or as a music director at a local church. We added two more sons, Nicholas and Jonathan, to our household. We progressed out of my parents' home and into an apartment, then to a rented house in suburbia, and finally to our first purchased home 40 miles from nowhere.

I quickly excelled and moved past the night shift and was promoted to an eight-to-five, Monday through Friday, pulmonary rehabilitation position. I was now wearing a dress shirt and necktie. I conversed easily with physicians and other professional staff members. I was presenting each month at the new employees' orientation for a large hospital. I saw a need and created a three-part workshop for parents of asthmatic children that was utilized years after I left the field.

**You can uncover, create, and
capitalize on your refining moments.**

I learned to uncover, create, and capitalize on refining moments, and I developed my own career path. But what do you do when you feel you have peaked in your career and you are only 27? What do you do when you feel you have so much more to offer and so much more earnings potential?

You go back to the classified section of the Sunday newspaper.

CHAPTER 5

WELCOME TO CORPORATE AMERICA

A GROUP OF APPROXIMATELY 90 hopefuls filled a hotel conference room, some of the best-looking, smartest, and brightness I'd ever seen. I wondered how many of them felt like I did when they read the large advertisement in the Sunday paper that read something along the lines of: Seeking highly driven, self-motivated, personable individuals who have experienced success in their career and are looking for the next opportunity that will reward them for their efforts.

The ad described me to a tee. This is what I had been searching for—a company that would see in me what I saw in myself, a company that would provide me with a formal training program, a company with name recognition and where the sky is the limit.

The advertisement was seeking prospective financial consultants for one of the nation's premier investment firms, Merrill Lynch, Pierce, Fenner and Smith Inc. What did I know about investments? Not much. Occasionally, I would pick up a copy of the *Wall Street Journal*. It kind of made me feel important, and I enjoyed reading many of the articles. And it gave me a glimpse into a world I knew nothing about, as the ads were for products completely foreign to my lower-middle-class background.

We sat as a group and listened to presentations from management and successful financial consultants. One speaker, Rex, was a handsome former baseball player. (Years later I would hire his brother.) He was dynamic, impressive, and an eloquent presenter. And judging by his suit, it was apparent he was doing quite well. Another young man named William spoke. William was even younger than me. He shared how he had moved from Oregon and was hired fresh out of college, which was rare. He joined the firm and, as a result of his hard work, he was able to earn $90,000 during his first year of production! This was 1985, and I was lucky if I would make $30,000 as a respiratory therapist.

Toward the conclusion of the presentations, we were informed that should we be interested, we were to line up at the front of the room with our resume, and a two- to three-minute on-the-spot interview would be conducted. If we made the cut, we would be contacted for round two of the interview process.

While selling myself in two to three minutes was going to be a significant financially refining moment—and physically refining, in that I hoped I would not pass out—I would classify this as an emotionally refining moment. It was highly unlikely that my resume would earn me a trip to round two. Somehow, I needed to bring all my emotional strength, passion, and determination—my total emotional-spiritual well-being—to that interview.

I lined up in front of Rex, with what seemed like hundreds of better-qualified individuals. When it was my turn, he quickly glanced at my resume as we exchanged pleasantries, and he asked me a question about the Los Angeles Olympics. I had been selected to perform with 83 other pianists at the Opening Ceremony of the 1984 Los Angeles Olympics the year before. Our 84 grand pianos came out to the gasp of 90,000 spectators, including President Ronald Reagan, and a television audience of 1 billion. We were all dressed in powder-blue tuxedos with coattails and performed George Gershwin's "Rhapsody in Blue." The television camera actually caught a glimpse of me performing. (Thanks to the contributions of family and friends, I still have the Olympic piano that I used to perform on that beautiful summer day.)

So my musical experience was going to be the launching point for my brief interview. Somehow I had to translate my training, perseverance, and limited success in music to a business career while bringing out a positive, dynamic personality of success. There was nothing else on my resume that was going to get me to round two.

I smiled and spoke briefly about the Olympics experience. I shared how I had quickly progressed in the field of respiratory therapy. And I said that this opportunity jumped right off the newspaper page and defined the person I know me to be and the professional I know I can become.

When the call for round two came, I could hardly believe it; then again, somehow I could. I met with a branch manager who was far less enthusiastic than the presenters at the hotel. In fact, he appeared almost too bored and important to meet with me. The interview did not seem to be going well, until he made a comment about just how hard this job was going to be. He seemed to insinuate that I had no appreciation of the investment of time and energy required. "This is not your usual nine-to-five job," he said.

> **This is not your usual nine-to-five job.**

Well, you can challenge me on my resume, my lack of sales or corporate experience, but you cannot challenge me on a lack of drive or work ethic! I literally snapped back about how hard I had to work just to get where I was, the example my dad set for us with his hard work ethic, the countless 16-hour shifts I pulled, never turning down an offer for overtime. I worked as a part-time music director at a local church, occasionally arriving on Sunday morning after working an all-night shift. "Hard work? I've worked the night shift and missed hours of sleep for over two years! I don't care how many hours I put in, if I get to come home and sleep next to my wife at night, anything else is easy!" I told him.

My comments seemed to capture his attention. I think that was another ERM. The manager woke up and saw the desire burning deep down in my soul.

And so I moved on to round three. I wore the same cheap suit as the previous two interviews and arrived at a penthouse office in Newport Beach, California. I was getting farther outside my comfort zone, completely out of my league. My appointment was with A.J., a Merrill Lynch complex manager with responsibilities over several offices. I had never met face-to-face with someone of his stature and level of success. A.J. was the epitome of a corporate America executive, and we met for close to one hour.

At the conclusion of our meeting, he smiled and, with a twinkle in his eye, explained that he was going to make an investment in me and send me to a corporate evaluation exercise in downtown Los Angeles. I would go through a corporate simulation with a group of other candidates for a couple of hours. We were going to play "broker for a day," and everything we did, wrote, and spoke was going to be observed and documented by a group of professionals. This exercise was going to cost him a few hundred dollars. If I passed and was selected to join the company, I would be assigned to a local office for a four-month training program, culminating in a three-week training session in New York with an opportunity to visit the floor of the New York Stock Exchange. During the training program, I would have one chance to pass each regulatory examination; if I failed any one test, I would be removed from the program. But to do all this, I would have to quit my job as a respiratory therapist.

Becky was worried and anxious, and, admittedly, so was I.

With a limited educational background, I probably studied harder than any other trainee. And I passed every examination, attended the New York training program, joined the firm, and took advantage of continued educational development opportunities. They were grooming me from the ground up for a lifetime career. My industry knowledge and level of confidence grew by leaps and bounds. As a family, we began dressing a bit better than we used to and occasionally we went out to some nicer restaurants. My physical, emotional, and financial strength grew more than my wife or I could ever have imagined. For better and sometimes worse, I began to change as a person.

> **For better and sometimes worse,
> I began to change as a person.**

Within 3 years, I had an opportunity to join a firm that was launching an investment program with a major bank.

I loved my career at Merrill Lynch but felt that I could make more money in a shorter amount of time, allowing me more time at home with our young family. I took the job, experienced recognition and success, bought a nice little Mercedes Benz, dressed even nicer, bought a bigger home, and progressed to my first management position in less than two years.

Over the next 10 years with the same company, there were a variety of vice president positions, six-figure incomes, corporate travel, recognition trips, black-tie events, and meeting celebrities and corporate leaders throughout America. I met the best of the best, politicians, and a U.S. president. It was a great ride, with refining moments too numerous to count. I kept my job when the company experienced a merger, and I assumed more responsibility. I lived in a beautiful home, drove a nice car, wore the finest of suits, and wore an executive wristwatch and an upgraded wedding ring; the kids had the latest gadgets and trendiest clothes; and Becky dressed at a level she never thought possible.

A life-changing physically refining moment arrived at the doctor's office when I learned I had a condition known as serous retinopathy. I was losing my eyesight. The doctor was quite surprised when he made the diagnosis. This was a condition usually seen in a much older population or in movie stars and athletes—those with megadoses of success and stress. Yet here I was, 34 years old and at a significant level of financial success, and my physician is taking steps to prevent blindness caused by stress.

I was also gaining weight and experiencing sleep issues. Physically, I was becoming a mess. I was going at such a fast pace that I wasn't taking time to reflect on PRMs or ERMs. I was fighting self-doubt, fear, and "if only people knew the real me" feelings related to a fear of success. My marriage and relationship with my sons began to suffer. The harmful physically and emotionally refining moments were having a direct impact on my prospects for continued employment and, ultimately, on our finances.

As a family, we had to take back control of our lives, rediscover our purpose, and make the appropriate refinements or course corrections. I needed to seek advice and assistance from others. I needed to come back to my childlike faith in my God and myself. But I also wasn't ready to leave corporate America. The previous 12 years did much to prepare me for the challenges I would face during my next 16 years in the finance world.

In my management positions going forward, I decided to focus more on coaching others toward well-rounded success and not just on sales results. I needed to shed the arrogance I had been developing and learn to serve others with principle-guided leadership. Eventually I would work with smaller companies than I had been doing. Coming to the brink of failure caused me to realize that there were countless others just like me—people too strong and prideful to admit they needed help or assistance. I survived, and I wanted others to survive and thrive alongside me.

I had worked in an environment where team members were pitted against each other. While this brought some short-term lift in the goals we were attempting to accomplish, my experience showed that creating an environment where team members seek the best for others and learn from each other brings even higher levels of performance and longer-term, consistent sales and investment results. We spend far too much time living and breathing with our "corporate family." It only made sense that we invest time, energy, and passion in our "corporate siblings," lest we end up with yet another dysfunctional corporate family.

The last several years of my corporate career, which ended in early 2013, were just as challenging as the early years—successes and setbacks, employment and unemployment, relocations, redefining my career path. But my life purpose, what truly motivates and inspires me, has become moving people farther along in terms of their physical, financial, and emotional-relational-spiritual well-being. This leads to more strength, stamina, achievement, and victory in life.

When you approach your life and career from this perspective, why on earth would you ever choose to retire? Retirement means to go away or sit

Why on earth would you ever choose to retire?

life out on the sidelines. By living a life of continuous improvement, you will always have something to offer someone or some organization.

My 28 years in corporate America revolved around the world of finance and investing. But here's a hot investment tip: We first need to invest in ourselves, financially, physically, and emotionally. Here's another tip: The investment return for investing in us is greatly multiplied in the lives of others.

Living a life of refinement—a life of continuous improvement—guides us toward living a life of greater purpose, greater impact, and a legacy with generational results.

To experience success, you must progress.

SECTION II

EMOTIONAL REFINEMENT

CHAPTER 6

THE BENEFITS OF A LEARNING VS. A PERFORMANCE ORIENTATION

DID YOU KNOW THERE ARE more women entering and finishing college than men? Or that there are more women starting small businesses than men? Women are taking over the world, especially the business world, and men, we may have some learnin' to do.

Women are taking over the world.

Over the years, I have had the opportunity to hire some of the best and the brightest financial advisors from across the country. I have observed and celebrated with those who overcame the odds in an extremely competitive profession and succeeded.

A few years into my management career, I began to notice a trend among our financial professionals. At many of our annual award conferences, there was a disproportionate number of female advisors at the front of the room receiving the awards and accolades for their performance and results. By disproportionate, I mean relative to the percentage of female versus male advisors. I have observed some very successful female advisors, with their passion and drive for success, run circles around their male counterparts in a male-dominated profession. In fact, female advisors have become one of my secret weapons for building a sales team that surpasses other regions within an organization.

I remember while interviewing for a leadership role with a new company, I asked the hiring manager, "What is the percentage of female advisors within this region?" The manager had to stop and think about it for a while, and then he responded, "Twelve, 15, maybe 20 percent. Why do you ask?" I simply responded, "Oh I'm typically used to managing a group more along the lines of 40, closer to 50 percent."

Perhaps, in our world of political correctness, we have become too cautious in discussing the role of gender in the workplace, but there are traits and skill sets that tend to be more dominant in each sex. We all have an opportunity to learn and refine our less-dominant skill set, and I am a firm believer that maturity has less to do with age and more to do with our ability to maximize both sides of our brain.

Many female workers, managers, and executives had to work very hard to fit in to a "man's world." I think the tables are turning, and we men better learn more about competing—not in a man's world, but in a "balanced world" in terms of our careers and personal relationships.

With more than one of the key female advisors I've hired in the past, I have joked—or, more truthfully, planted the seed: Remember me when you make it to the top! Being the intelligent man that I am, I know there is a good chance that one day I could be coming to one of my former advisors for employment.

I feel fortunate to have lived during a critical transition from a technical, operational, military, or sports-inspired management model (all male-dominated) to the information (gender-neutral) age. Think of the some of the common business jargon that has been in place for years and springs from male vernacular: team member, team captain, par for the course, guerrilla marketing, home run, full-court press. Men who did well in sports or military careers were naturally assumed to go on to have a successful career or be a great leader. But it is my observation that in this information age, many women tend to have an advantage. So, women, run with it! Continue to develop your skill set and you will be rewarded.

The great news for men is, it is never too late. With some effort, men can continue to compete and succeed in the career world, and foster more rewarding and meaningful relation-

Continue to develop your skill set and you will be rewarded.

ships. And, with good fortune, the female CEO will consider us a key part of her group!

A PERFORMANCE ORIENTATION

During the 1990s, I experienced some mind-boggling swings in my career. Corporate mergers—true and rumored—surrounded the financial services and banking industry. If you did not have a fight-or-flight mentality before, you certainly developed one during this decade. There is one position that I held, more of a one-year project, at Bank of America, with the title of vice president of future markets. With the title came somewhat of a vague job description (my forte), but this group was charged with assessing and harnessing the resources of a 50,000-employee organization toward capitalizing on various market segments including Hispanic, African American, Asian, women, and the aging population. The theory was, the more we know about some potentially underserved groups, the more appropriately we can serve and attract key market segments. Better products and services equaled more profits.

There were times during this assignment that I wondered what I was doing there. I was off the front lines of direct sales and management, out of my comfort zone. Little did I know there would be numerous refining moments that would arise and shape my career and life during this one-year assignment.

Because our work was closely aligned with behavioral patterns and future trends in our industry and society as a whole, I was selected to attend a seminar workshop for men—more specifically, male managers—titled "Efficacy for Men." I was told that the workshop was a pilot program, and I would join a group of around 20 men, all vice presidents and above, from various parts of the organization. We would fly to the firm's training facility, be housed in corporate condos for a few days, and return 30 days later for a follow-up workshop.

The first day of our training session started out as most, with basic male chitchat on sports, weather, title, and position. Although we won't admit it, what men are actually doing is quickly accessing our male competition and determining who's who in the corporate pecking order. With 20 male execs, you can spot the dominant alpha male type ("probably came up through sales"); the less alpha, more intelligent male ("probably a finance guy"); and the well-dressed, colorfully attired man ("marketing").

You may not want to admit it, but we all have our stereotypes.

You may not want to admit it, but we all have our stereotypes.

Again, none of us attendees had a true understanding of why we were selected or what the workshop would entail. So, while we were all joking around, shooting the breeze, there was some sense of uneasiness among our group.

At the front of the room, there were three workshop facilitators and, after some brief introductions and a vague but general overview of the curriculum, the lead facilitator started off the session with a simple question: "Men, what comes to mind when you think of men?"

We were all a little confused, so he repeated the question as he walked to a flipchart to record our responses. Finally someone says "smart." Someone else offers "tough." This kicks off additional responses, and pretty soon we had a couple of pages with words such as:

- Aggressive
- Decisive
- Results-oriented
- Take-charge
- Strong
- Power
- Boss
- My way or the highway

Then the facilitator walked over to a flipchart on the other side of the room and asked, "Okay men, what comes to mind when you think of women?"

"Now we're talking!" expressions and glances crisscrossed the room, along with whispered comments and jokes. The facilitator calmed us down and repeated the question, slowly and deliberately. Our responses were:

- Soft
- Listening

- Intuitive
- Communicative
- Sixth sense
- Caring
- Dedicated

And the list went on.

Then the facilitator stepped back with his arms outstretched, pointing to the two flipcharts, and asked a simple, yet powerful question that I will never, ever forget. "Men, as we are going into this next century, which skill set do you think corporate America is looking for in their managers and leadership teams?"

Which skill set do you think corporate America is looking for in their managers and leadership teams?"

Bamm! I had been witnessing a transition in corporate America, and now someone had the courage to talk about it.

With continued discussion and training, it became apparent that the traditional male-dominant skill set or approach to management was suitable for war—"Charge that hill!"—or for technical or operational environments—"Turn this valve when the temperature hits 180 degrees!"—but less fitting in this information age. The days of the boss barking out orders and handing out assignments, and the subordinates following these orders with no questions asked, were changing.

I was already beginning to observe these changes, especially within the commoditized world of financial services. When I first started out as a broker at Merrill Lynch, if you wanted a stock quote, you had to call us. As brokers, we controlled the flow of information, and information combined with knowledge was power. As a man, like my other colleagues, I loved that sense of power. Nowadays, you can basically open a checking account, get a loan, and buy a stock or mutual fund anywhere anytime. The world has changed, but many of our patterns of development and training have not.

The world has changed, but many of our patterns of development and training have not.

As we continued with our training session, we discussed our relationship with our fathers, our fears, our concerns surrounding our need to compete, our need to prove ourselves and not show emotion, and our continuous drive for recognition, affirmation, and success. We discussed our childhood and common patterns of development. To this day, I have never participated in anything as heavy or as deep an emotional topic within a corporate environment. I do not know if this pilot program was ever offered again within the organization, but I can honestly state that this was probably one of the most significant refining moments of my career.

I caution you: the following may come across as stereotypical. However, let me relate to you some aspects of my childhood, which of course laid the groundwork or patterns of development for my future career in management.

It's the mid-1960s, and early on I had expressed interest in learning how to play my mom's piano. So my parents made the sacrifice to pay for piano lessons. This meant, whether I wanted to or not, I had to practice at least 30 minutes a day, an early lesson in training, effort, and results.

On any given day, my friends would knock on the front door and ask me to come out and play. There was no way I was going to refuse this invitation, nor was I going to tell the guys, "No, I have to practice the piano" or "I have to vacuum my room." So my answer was always "Sure!"

On one particular day, I headed outside with my buddies, and the guys said, "We're going to play football." And I thought, *Oh no, here we go again: it is time to pick teams.*

The two captains took turns pointing out the guys they wanted to select for their teams. As a guy, you shrink more and more as you await the selective finger to be pointed in your direction. (Do you see a future career pattern developing here? Have you ever worked for a guy that you are convinced must have always been picked last?)

Once the teams were picked, we went into our respective huddles. "Hey Greg, can you go out for a long bomb (a long pass)?" I was asked.

Without any hesitation, I quickly replied, "Heck yeah, of course I can!"

Deep down, though, I was thinking, *Oh man, I hope I can. I'm not the best football player, but I can't say no, and if I hurt my piano fingers, my mom is going to kill me!*

Then came the do-not-question-authority instructions from the quarterback: "You guys go here, and you guys go there, Greg you run there and turn. Ready?"

We all shouted back, "Ready!"

"Set, set, hike!" We all burst forward, and I was running as fast as my skinny little legs would carry me, and the ball was thrown …

Now, perhaps, this is a spiritual refining moment because I was praying just as hard as I was running. *Please let me catch it, oh Lord, please let me catch it! Because if I catch the ball, even if it is a lucky catch, I am a winner, I am a hero, we will all dance in the end zone, and the guys will be so impressed! If I drop the ball, I am a loser, I am a failure, the guys will be mad, and I will never be picked for the team again.*

For me, this story helps illustrate what Dr. Carol Leggett refers to as a performance orientation. In a performance orientation pattern of development, there are

> **You wonder if your abilities are adequate, and you must always prove yourself.**

winners and there are losers. You wonder if your abilities are adequate, and you must always prove yourself. You face challenging situations with questions like "Can I do it?" or "Will I look smart?" When faced with uncertainty, you feel threatened. You seek flattering versus accurate information.

A LEARNING ORIENTATION

When I was young, on any given day, I would observe my little sister Lucy with her friends.

"What are you doing?" I'd ask.

"We're playing tea" or "We're baking brownies" or "We are playing with our dolls."

I'd observe their playtime for less than a minute (boring) and ask, "I don't get it. Who is winning?"

"Who's winning?" my sister would sharply reply. "There are no winners, there are no losers. We are visiting!"

Huh?

Again, perhaps this is stereotypical, but go back to that same football huddle. If Lucy and her friends were in it, the dialogue might have gone something like this.

"Okay, gather around girls. Isn't it a lovely day? Let's see what we can accomplish." To which they would all take turns replying and sharing their thoughts on the lovely day. Several minutes later, the huddle dialogue would continue.

"So I am thinking of throwing a long forward pass, Lucy. What do you think? Would you like to go out for a pass?"

Lucy responds, "You know what, Jane, I would love to because I have experienced success with this endeavor so many times before and, therefore, I am fully confident I have the ability to catch the ball. But, today, I am just not myself. I have noticed Sally is having a pretty good day, so why don't we ask Sally?"

Jane responds, "Thank you for sharing, Lucy, and we all appreciate your valuable, yet candid feedback. Okay, Sally, what do you think? Would you like to go out for a pass?"

Sally enthusiastically replies, "Absolutely! I have caught the ball on several occasions, and today I am having an exceptional day. Thank you, girls, for noticing!"

For me, this exaggeration helps to illustrate what Dr. Leggett refers to as a learning orientation. It is not that someone with a learning orientation has more or less of a desire to compete and succeed in obtaining a goal than someone with a performance orientation. It is more of a mind-set on approaching the goal, your gathering of meaningful information, and your response to potential setbacks.

"How can I do it?" versus "Can I do it?"

In a learning orientation, the question is "How can I do it?" versus "Can I do it?" When faced with uncertainty, you feel challenged, not threatened. You seek accurate information versus flattering information. If you miss the mark or goal, you are not a loser; you simply ask yourself, "What information do I need to do better next time?"

This question bears repeating because this is the question you should continue to ask as you read through this book and every single day:

What information do I need to do better next time?

Let me share with you a realistic example of a performance orientation mentality and a very practical example of implementing what we learned from this training. I can recall the facilitator closing one of our sessions with the following exercise: "Men, I know this is a lot to take in, and some of you are having difficulty in comprehending these concepts. So I am going to share some words with you that can have a profound impact on your life. Repeat after me: I am wrong. You are right. I am sorry."

Someone in your life needs to hear those spoken words.

The concepts we learned and those simple words brought some tears to our eyes when we returned 30 days later for the follow-up training session. Many of us shared with the group how we began to apply these concepts first in our home, then in our workplace. Many of us examined the excess baggage and the chip on our shoulder that drove much of our behavior in both places.

Following the first training session, I shared with my skeptical wife the concepts I had learned and my desire to improve. I sat down with my three sons and told them, "You need to know I am so proud of you. You are very important to me. I act as if I have it all together and like I don't make any mistakes. Half the time, I am scared to death and I don't always know what I am doing. I push you guys hard because I don't want you to make the same mistakes I have made, but you need to know, we are all in this together. I am sorry for coming across so critical at times. You boys are great, and I love you!"

A learning orientation versus a performance orientation. This emotionally refining moment was significant and probably key to why I am writing this today. Once you capture and absorb this concept, your life will never be the same.

In the years following my training in this area, I have used these concepts to better evaluate potential employees. On numerous occasions, I have interviewed potential employees and listened as the applicant bashed his former employer and demonstrated a cockiness, a persona of "I'm the greatest and you should feel lucky to hire me." And I think, "Poor guy, he is so PO'd (performance oriented)."

Give me an employee who strives for success, has a qualified sense of self-confidence, and is willing to seek input and course correction when appropriate.

Give me an employee, a business partner, or a corporation that will continuously ask, "What information do I/we need to do better the next time?"

"I am wrong. You are right. I am sorry."

If we are going to refine our lives, many of us need to address the topic of seeking and accepting forgiveness. We can go a lifetime holding resentment for being wounded or wronged, and this will have a detrimental physical and emotional impact on our lives. More than likely, a lifelong feeling of resentment can have a negative impact on our career and finances as well. Our actions or lack of seeking forgiveness can have a tremendous negative impact on those we interact with.

> **I am wrong.
> You are right.
> I am sorry.**

Could it be that your employees or co-workers ignore much of what you say because they have no respect for you? Does your inability to admit your mistakes place a concrete barrier between you and your spouse, significant other, or children? Are there relationships that could be salvaged by addressing your mistakes and offering a sincere apology?

In a song popular in the '60s are the words, "What the world needs now is love, sweet love." I say, what the world needs now is forgiveness—to forgive and to seek forgiveness; a world with no regrets.

To forgive and to seek forgiveness; a world with no regrets.

If you desire to have close, personal relationships, if you want to earn the respect of your peers, if you want to positively impact those you love, then we need to get this right:

Pick up the phone, or

Get out a pen and paper, or

Sit down face-to-face and talk.

If you have been wronged, you might approach the person and request a dialogue of reconciliation. If this is not possible, let it go, discuss your situation with a trusted friend or advisor, or seek professional assistance to deal with the hurt and the pain.

Refinement means sifting through the issue, eliminating the toxic elements, and creating a stronger, more improved you. Set the example for your workplace, your loved ones, and those within your world.

CHAPTER 7

PRIDE

NOW HERE'S A SUBJECT I know something about. Why wouldn't I be proud? I am proud of the distance traveled from where I started. I am proud of my accomplishments in the corporate world and in the field of music. I am proud of my three sons. I am proud of my country. And the list goes on.

So when does pride become a hindrance or an obstacle to a life of refinement and continuous improvement? Aren't pride and self-esteem vital ingredients in any recipe for success?

Once again, what we are attempting to accomplish is the identification of toxic versus nontoxic ingredients. Consider for a moment an ugly piece of ore, basically a rock. This ugly rock can undergo a process of refinement, separating the useless from the beneficial elements and be transformed into a beautiful piece of stainless steel. This stainless steel can then be refined or transformed into a valuable wristwatch or a surgical instrument. So what started as a rock is now something fit for use.

So it goes with the attribute of pride. There is the toxic kind—pride that is detrimental to our relationships and personal life of refinement—and there is nontoxic pride that is fit for use.

In his book, *The Man in the Mirror: Solving the 24 Problems Men Face*, Patrick Morley describes two types of pride:

- A pride based on self-examination. We can take pride in ourselves based on our own actions, effort, and accomplishments.
- A pride based on a feeling of superiority in which we compare our strengths to another individual's weaknesses. We elevate our own self-worth by putting other people down verbally or mentally. Morley quotes C. S. Lewis: "A proud man is always looking down on things and people; and, of course, as long as you're looking down, you can't see something that's above you."

Have you observed in others or yourself evidence of toxic pride? Have you witnessed the negative ramifications in personal relationships or on career paths in the workplace?

Competition and comparison is something we can all relate to.

Competition and comparison is something we can all relate to. When applied for the right reasons, I believe a dose of competition and comparison fuels improvement opportunities—sort of like jet fuel for inspiration, imagination, and invention. For example, you know there are gifted scientists and biotech corporations trying to find a cure for cancer; while I am confident doing so would bring monetary rewards, society as a whole has benefited from the competition to discover lifesaving medical solutions. These scientists should be proud of their efforts.

I love to compete and compare myself to others in the workplace. The posting of regional and individual sales results is a part of my corporate landscape. When you see an employee who has always lagged the group suddenly shoot past everyone for three months in a row, you should be comparing and inquiring as to the reasons for her success. Everyone else has an opportunity to discover the bar has moved higher, and by adopting some new success strategies, we too can move to even higher levels of performance.

So when does competition, comparison, or a prideful nature become toxic? For me, it has been when I cannot seem to turn it off—when I am being prideful to cover my own sense of insecurity, or when I am simply comparing myself to others, not to learn but to artificially boost my self-esteem or ego.

Let me give you an example. Did you know I am the smartest driver on the road, especially during adverse road conditions? I know the *exact* speed limit to drive at any given time, not more, not less. Let's say snow is starting to fall during my morning commute, and as I pull onto the highway, I get stuck behind someone driving too slowly.

"Come on, speed it up, the snow is not that bad," I'll say to myself. When I have the opportunity, I pass the car, maybe tap on my horn to acknowledge my frustration, and continue with my commute. "Wimpy driver!"

Suddenly another car seems to appear out of nowhere and zooms up right on my tail.

"Did he just flash his lights at me?"

As the car whizzes past me, I'm thinking, "What a jerk, he's driving way too fast. With those cheap tires on that piece-of-junk car, he'll probably spin off the road. Idiot! I hope you get a speeding ticket!"

Now, I would like to think that I am experiencing genuine concern for the other driver's safety. Truth be told, I am angry and ticked off because he's not smart enough to determine the optimal speed for the current road conditions. This idiot just challenged my male pride and ego. He is accusing me of being a wimp.

And that is just the first negative comparison of my day.

"What a goof. He just doesn't get it."

"That suit, tie, and haircut are so 1980s."

"That person seems to lack self-confidence. No real social skills."

"You think she'd be further along in her career by now."

Toxic forms of pride can be outright ugly. If we truly examine our motive when comparing ourselves to others, more often than not it is to boost our own sense of self-worth at the expense of others. Going back to a performance-versus-learning orientation, rather than learning what we can from any given situation, we settle for a quick fix of feeling better, rather than getting better or aiming for continuous improvement.

Toxic forms of pride can be outright ugly.

Did you feel you were entitled to the next promotion and were wrongly passed up? Your internal dialogue of comparison might sound something like this:

"Why did she get the job? Everyone knows I could do it better. She always seems nervous in front of a group, and I am a much better presenter. I have more years of experience, and I have held similar positions in the past. She must not have a life, and the company knows she will live and breathe this job. I am not going to sell myself out for this company. Overall, I am a much better person and I have the friends to prove it."

There's a good dose of pride and toxic comparison. While some of my self-assessment may seem valid, you can bet money I will verify it with my friends or close business associates.

How much more could I learn if I conclude my internal dialogue as follows:

"Wow, I didn't get the job and she did? It should have been me. I have proven skills for the position. But what else was management considering when they selected her? I know I am a talented presenter. Maybe her experience in marketing was a key issue? Could it be the company would like to expand in a different direction and she brings a stronger overall skill set? I need to sit down with her, offer my congratulations, and seek her input on the direction of the company. I need to make sure the leadership team is aware that I am willing to develop my skill set and adapt to a new strategic course. I need to seek their input on how I can continue to develop my strengths and overcome any perceived weaknesses, so that I can continue to contribute in a meaningful way."

Easier said than done? Perhaps. But refining attitudes about pride from life is a worthy goal.

I believe toxic pride is habit forming and harmful to your closest relationships and your reputation in the workplace. I am sure there are countless times my children overheard my negativity toward others, putting someone down, artificially boosting my own self-worth. Fortunately, looking at my sons in their adulthood, I feel they have learned from observing me, as they seem to demonstrate more grace toward those I may have marginalized in the past.

And when a prideful person falls from the corporate ladder, those he negatively compared himself to along the way likely won't care.

The challenge is for all of us to continually exam our own motives.

The challenge is for all of us to continually exam our own motives. Better yet, we should seek input from a trusted family member, mentor, or friend. Ask for forgiveness, if appropriate, and share your desire to slay the dragon of toxic pride.

ERM: Take inventory of things you are proud of: home, job, appearance, status, travel, family, education, skill set, etc. Next to each item, list the toxic and nontoxic elements associated with your pride for each item. Strive to eliminate the negative and grow the positive. At the end, be proud of yourself for taking the time to complete this exercise!

CHAPTER 8

ANGER

IS THIS A SUBJECT I know something about? Could it be that I am somewhat of an expert on the topic of anger? Unfortunately, the answer is yes.

While the topics chosen for this ERM section can have a profound negative impact on our ability to develop long-lasting, meaningful, trusted relationships, these topics are not limited to ERM alone. In my own experience, and in observing hundreds of successful and less-fortunate executives, I can attest that the issues presented can have a significantly negative impact on our FRM and PRM as well.

Such is the case with anger. Many of us can think of "successful" individuals who are known for their anger or explosive behavior. But what is the cost of this display of emotion? What is the toll on their relational life and physical health? How much more successful could they be if they chose to effectively manage their anger?

Once again, I believe there are toxic and nontoxic forms of anger. Anger or the expression of frustration with the lack of progress toward a worthy goal can motivate you and others to pick up the pace, get past any barriers, and get the project completed. Getting angry with your children, for the right reasons, can help teach them to properly prioritize their responsibilities and tasks, which in turn can help them remember to complete their homework before going outside to play.

I would *like* to say that, for the most part, when I am angry or express my frustration, my motives have been pure, with a desire to bring out the best in others; but this is simply not the case. I have had to deal with toxic anger, and it ranks right up there as an emotional characteristic that can have a profound, negative impact on your financial and physical health. Sooner or later, your toxic anger will take its toll. Anger is like a concrete roadblock in your path of refinement.

Anger is like a concrete roadblock in your path of refinement.

In his book, *Anger Management: 6 Critical Steps to a Calmer Life*, author Peter Favaro, PhD, compares anger to an overheated car radiator ready to blow its top. Every individual has only so much room for frustration and displeasure before they reach a boiling point. That point is reached, too, when our attempts to seek pleasure are blocked or frustrated.

As a rookie manager (and rookie dad, for that matter), I often found myself very frustrated and ready to boil at a moment's notice. Looking back, I recognize that rarely was there one particular situation that would cause me to boil over; more often than not, I was already halfway there.

Bad day at the office? Watch out, kids.

Bad day at home? Watch out, employees.

Unfortunately for our families and our closest personal relationships, the job usually wins. You can't say what you really want to say or act out in a manner that causes you to lose your job, so you fill up your inner imaginary radiator and overheat at the end of the day around those you love the most.

Much of my own frustration revolved around my attempts to be a perfect boss and have a perfect family. Anything that caused me displeasure in my attempts toward this "perfection" caused me to be angry. When I really dug down deep, the person I was most angry and frustrated with was me. I will continue to refine and manage my anger like those I have admired over the years:

- The supervisor who does not fly off the handle, but takes sufficient time to evaluate a situation from various perspectives and responds appropriately.

- The loving parent who helps their children determine for themselves what they've done wrong and the consequences of their behavior, and then assigns appropriate corrective action.
- The coach who always finds something to praise his athletes for before offering up an improvement opportunity.

My family will acknowledge that I have improved tremendously over the years, but I must admit there is more room for growth and refinement. Identifying and learning from your emotionally, physically, and financially refining moments in life will be extremely difficult if you are in a state of anger.

ERM: Identify the triggers that make you angry. Seek to eliminate or better manage those triggers and list some coping strategies. Consider additional resources such as books or stress management techniques, or seek professional assistance to break down the concrete barrier of anger.

CHAPTER 9

ATTITUDE

IN CHAPTER 4, I PROVIDED a simple equation that profoundly defines our attitude:

Gratitude + Expectation = Attitude

Think for a moment just how critical our attitude is to our emotional-relational-spiritual state, along with the implications for our health and financial well-being. Let's break down the two components to the equation.

GRATITUDE

"When you are discouraged ... with a load of care ... Count your blessings, name them one by one, count your blessings, see what God hath done."

These are the words from an old hymn that I heard sung as a child in a small country-like church. Some might cynically think, "Oh that song is a crutch," but I observed firsthand the positive impact it had on the people around me, including my mother. She has lived and continues to exemplify a life of gratitude, expectation, and positive attitude. You might say gratitude is in my DNA. Oh sure, I can worry and complain with the best of them; but at my core is a lifelong sense of gratitude. When I would complain or doubt my ability to compete, my mom would remind me of how I have been blessed in the past and I have the resources to continue to be blessed in the future. "Son, you have so much to be grateful for," she would say.

These words were put to the test when I first launched my career as a financial consultant. I was on commission with a family to feed, and fear would creep into my mind. "Am I really going to make it in this business? Why couldn't I come from a family of money with wealthy contacts?"

I had to stop my negativity. After much reflection, I came to the calming conclusion that if this is as good as it gets—my current income, my family, and my current home—I would be satisfied knowing I have been blessed!

Now, this certainly didn't mean that I was not going to work hard or would stop working my way up the corporate ladder. I just needed to put my mind and attitude at ease with the understanding that I have been blessed and that I am truly grateful for each step up the corporate ladder. When you are climbing that ladder, you never know if yesterday's step was as high as you are going to climb. So you'd better take time at the end of each day to reflect with gratefulness for the opportunities and the accomplishments of that given day.

The same holds true with the ladder of relationships and physical health: at the end of each day, reflect and count your blessings.

> **You never know if yesterday's step was as high as you are going to climb.**

EXPECTATION

"Something good is going to happen to you …" The words of yet another song I heard growing up.

A daily dose of positive expectation fuels a life of refinement. A process of refinement, by its very nature, means something better is just around the corner. Oh sure, we all hit some bumps in the road, and some of life's bumps can turn out to be absolute mountains; but, if we recognize these negative experiences as refining moments, we can acknowledge that these moments better shape and prepare us for life in general. Your recovery from today's trial could be of benefit to someone else going through the same situation in the future.

A child who grows up in a loving and nurturing environment has an infinite capacity to get back up from a fall, dust off, and go back to playing. In no time at all, the child is laughing and facing life with innocence and optimism. Why is it that many people outgrow their childhood optimism? I am not saying all of us need to walk around with a goofy smile, holding daisies and greeting everyone we meet with a proclamation of "Today is a great day!" For most of us, that's just not in our nature. But I do believe that, if we consciously consider all that we have to be grateful for, even if it's just waking up alive, we can approach the day with an internal, almost giddy sense of expectation that something good is just around the corner.

The "good" may not mean a job promotion or a new car; it may simply mean a new acquaintance, someone recognizing your accomplishments, or reconnecting with a former colleague. The good might be your child experiencing success in a new endeavor.

> **We can approach the day with an internal, almost giddy sense of expectation.**

The good may also be a significant refining moment disguised as today's challenge or obstacle. If you train yourself to be on the lookout for a refining moment, you can't help but face each day with a childlike sense of hope, optimism, and expectation.

Something good is going to happen today!

ERM: Journal your day's activity and record the "good" of the day and the potentially refining moment for good in the future.

CHAPTER 10

SPIRITUALITY

HAVING WORKED IN THE CORPORATE world for my entire adult life, I often find it easier to relate concepts in a manner appropriate to a corporate setting or business audience. While this is not a book devoted to spiritual awareness or growth, I believe there is no way to address your total emotional well-being without considering the topic of spirituality. I believe a development of your personal spiritual life is vital to living a life of refinement and continuous improvement. Now, if this does not sound like you, please don't turn away from this topic. As you will see, I've purposely addressed this in a broader, general manner that should be of benefit to all.

As a manager in the workplace, I am all too aware of what is considered politically correct and what topics are considered appropriate within the realm of acceptable conversation. But if we truly have a desire to connect with others on a higher, more fulfilling emotional level, the topic of spirituality is bound to come up. So let me share with you some thoughts of a practical nature.

THE FIVE FS

When I was a rookie financial consultant, I came across an article in a trade journal written by a stockbroker and, although I never purchased or read his book, Jim Harnsberger's article had a significant influence on my life. It listed his priorities in life as the Five Fs: Faith, Family, Friends, Fitness, and Finance.

A few years later, I was a sales manager, and my wife and I hosted our first holiday dinner for my group of employees. It was your usual annual recognition type of event at a nice hotel. I felt compelled to share a few words about the holidays because I believe "He is the reason for the season," but in no way did I want to offend anyone since I was representing a corporation and the corporation was covering the cost of the event. So I chose to share the concept of the Five Fs.

I acknowledged the top producers, thanked our entire group, as well as those who supported them, and then I began. "Faith, Family, Friends, Fitness, and Finance. We live in a day and age where it is not considered appropriate to talk about your faith. Some of you may know or have figured out that my faith plays an important role in my life, and, if you are interested, you are welcome to

ask me more and I will be happy to share my personal thoughts and beliefs. You need not share the same faith as me, and some of you may feel you have no "formal" faith. But you can still prioritize your life with faith in your skills, your talent, your past experiences, and your abilities. I challenge you to write down what motivates you and why you have confidence in doing what you do."
I went on to share some thoughts on the remaining Fs.

People do want to connect on a higher level.

Did the message connect? Judging by their attentiveness, some heads nodding in agreement, a quieter moment of reflection, I knew I was on to something: people do want to connect on a higher level. People desire to be driven by something more than just a paycheck. Almost 20 years later, I was encouraged when an ERM came from seemingly nowhere. By chance, I crossed paths with a former employee, and he referenced that holiday evening and how he often reflected on the message of the Five Fs.

Over the years, as I've considered the power of faith in the workplace, I developed yet another simple illustration that I have shared with hundreds of financial advisors. I am certain that if you interviewed these individuals, many would be able to recall it: MOS and your Personal Board of Directors.

PERSONAL BOARD OF DIRECTORS

As I trained or interviewed financial consultants, I explained that in their personal practice, or territory, there were three key departments that needed to be fully operational at all times. If just one of these departments performed at an unsatisfactory level, their business would fail.

The Marketing Department (M): Identifying key target markets, raising product need awareness levels, generating referrals, being responsible for getting "cheeks in the seats."

The Operations Department (O): Managing paperwork, compliance requirements, legal disclosures, and day-to-day workflow, systems, and procedures.

The Sales Department (S): Knowing the product, industry, and financial markets; having an ability to present complex concepts in a simplified manner; establishing rapport; and closing sales.

I would then pose the question, "So guess who's the department head and manages each of these three departments?"

The answer is, you! This was the concept I developed that became known as MOS.

We would go on to discuss the importance of approaching the business as their own mini-corporation, with them holding the title of CEO in charge of their organization and the three key departments. It is the CEO's responsibility to evaluate the effectiveness of each business manager. If they had a high close ratio, that's great; it means their sales department is running at full speed. But if they were not seeing enough people in any given month, then they needed to have a talk with their "marketing manager" (themselves) and strategize some corrective action. This placed the responsibility for success and setbacks solely on their shoulders. They couldn't pass the buck and blame someone else.

I would then outline a corporate organizational chart (with the CEO over the marketing, operations, and sales departments). We would discuss some of the key tasks within each box, but before we concluded and outlined some appropriate action plans, I would remind the CEO that he or she does not operate in a vacuum. There is a board of directors that ultimately holds the entire organization, including the CEO, accountable on behalf of the shareholders. If you really want to succeed, you need to define your shareholders and your Personal Board of Directors (PBOD).

Who makes up your PBOD? For me, it includes my wife, my children, my grandchildren, and, ultimately, my God. When I want to slack off, back off, hide under a rock, or maybe cut a few corners, or when I need to make tough decisions such as letting someone go, I am comforted and driven by the fact that

Who makes up your Personal Board of Directors?

I am held accountable by a higher source or power. My PBOD is counting on me to do the right thing.

A life of refinement is so much easier when you fully understand why you do what you do; when you know your highest calling; and when you recognize the fact that you have been blessed with resources and have a responsibility to exploit, grow, and share those resources (or, as I often shared with our business team members, "maximize our franchise!").

ERM: Define your spirituality in terms of a Personal Board of Directors. To whom or what standard are you held accountable? Are you living up to your responsibilities? Are you a good steward and manager of what you have been entrusted with?

CHAPTER 11

MEANINGFUL CONVERSATIONS

WE HAVE ADDRESSED SOME OF the key emotional barriers that stifle our emotional skill set, such as anger and pride, and we addressed the importance of having a firm foundation of spirituality and faith. Now we are ready to continue the process of taking our relationships to a higher level. Let's put into practice some strategies for creating emotionally refining moments on a daily basis.

The first course of action is to take inventory of our various relationships, determine the quality of each relationship, and seek corrective measures or a course of action to advance each relationship to a higher level of mutual satisfaction and codependency. Yes, as challenging as it may seem to our pride or ego, we are and should be codependent with our significant relationships.

STEP 1: IDENTIFY RELATIONSHIPS

The obvious first is a spouse, significant other, or life partner.

Next are most likely our children, blended households, parents, in-laws, and other key familial relationships.

Then come friends, mentors, neighbors, co-workers, and associates. Some of these relationships may have priority over others and, while I am not asking you to rank your friends, know that close friends and associates could be more significant than some familial relationships in terms of mutual importance and dependency.

STEP 2: ASSESS THE QUALITY OF EACH RELATIONSHIP

Author and family psychologist Gary Smalley shares a process that my wife and I have utilized on different occasions. It is a simple question that goes something like this: "Honey, on a scale of 1 to 10, how would you rate our marriage right now, and where would you like it to be?"

If the answer to the first part of the question is less than 5, there is a good chance you could use some professional assistance or additional resources. If the answer is 6 and it used to be 8, it is time to take some corrective action. Your response to your spouse's answer might sound something along these lines, "So, if you feel we are at a 6 right now, what steps can we take to get it back up to a 7 or 8?

The answer might include a redistribution of household responsibilities, assistance with the children, planning a weekly date night, or simply taking time to listen to the stresses your partner is experiencing. Just the fact that you are even having this discussion greatly increases the odds that you will move forward in a favorable direction.

I remember meeting with a successful financial advisor who shared with me how he leads his clients through a similar exercise. During an initial client review, he will come right out and ask a couple to rate their marriage on a scale of 1 to 10. If together they uncover some key spousal issues, he will suggest allocating a sufficient source of funds for professional couples counseling before he will even consider investing their funds; otherwise, he feels he is simply building more assets for their lawyers to eventually split during divorce proceedings. Now, that's putting your money where your mouth is!

This same exercise on a scale of 1 to 10 can be beneficial with your children and other close personal relationships.

What about our relationships with co-workers, friends, and associates? Do we sit down and have the same conversation? It depends on the closeness of the relationship. But you can conduct your own assessment of where you are and where you could be.

I had the opportunity to get to know author and speaker Tommy Spaulding. He has observed and trained throughout corporate America on the importance of higher-level relationships in the workplace. In his book, *It's Not Just Who You Know*, he shares a concept of the "five floors" of relationships—rated from the first floor to the penthouse. First floor relationships are your typical news-weather-sports types of conversations (unfortunately, many of us don't get past these with our own children or other important relationships). He makes the case for a correlation between higher-level relationships in the workplace and increased profits.

STEP 3: MEANINGFUL CONVERSATIONS

So how do you take a relationship to a higher level? I believe it starts with our ability to have meaningful conversations. The basics of communication involve:

- A sender: someone speaking, as well as sending nonverbal communication
- A receiver: someone listening and accepting the delivered messages
- Filters: factors that influence and affect our ability to process the messages being sent and delivered (e.g., past experiences, previous conversations, etc.)

Truthfully, we are usually sending and receiving messages simultaneously. But let's focus on you as the sender. "Kids, clean up your room" can be delivered and received at so many different levels. If life is going well and you have sent plenty of constructive messages and there is harmony in your home, your children might internally respond, "Oh yeah, my room is messy and mom already asked me once. I better get to it."

If life is not going as well—you have been angry on the job, and you and your spouse have been going at it all week—there is a filter of tension when you deliver your message. And most likely, your children have experienced very little one-on-one conversations with you for the past several days. Consider how your clean-up message might be received and the internal dialogue taking place: "I can't do anything right. It's not my fault. All I do is keep messing up. I'm sick of cleaning my room and nobody seems to care when I do something right! I can't wait until I'm old enough to get the heck out of here!"

Consider how many messages we send and receive every single day at home or in the workplace. What steps can we take to improve our conversations?

What steps can we take to improve our conversations?

PLANTING AND WATERING SEEDS

Many of our interactions and conversations happen by chance. But if we think in terms of growing a healthy organic garden, I believe we can improve our level of communication and the significance of our relationships. Consider this Organic Garden Model of communication:

Planting seeds = The sending of messages

Watering the seeds = Listening and receiving or letting those seeds take root

Nourishing the seeds = Reducing or eliminating the toxic substances, filters, or barriers to our communication

As a supervisor, boss, manager, father, spouse, and author, I have eagerly planted numerous seeds far too many times. I love giving advice and sharing improvement opportunities. But if I'm so busy planting seeds, am I giving ample time to the watering process? Am I carefully paying attention to the nutrients of our conversation?

Here is a simple step or ERM that can greatly improve your relationship: while you are communicating, plant some seeds and then stop and shut up. Let those seeds take root, and let them be nourished by listening. Take time to assess how your seeds of communication have been received. Take time to let the other person speak, or water your seeds with their input.

Nourish your garden by feeding your conversations with positive responses, acknowledgments, and feedback. Eliminate the toxins such as jumping too quickly to a response or conclusion. Eliminate distractions and stop multitasking when you should be giving your undivided attention. One acquaintance shared with me how dramatically his interactions improved with his spouse when he simply made a conscious effort to always be looking at her when she speaks. I shudder to think what you would observe if all of my conversations were recorded with a hidden video camera: wandering eyes, a look of disinterest, checking the time, looking at my cell phone. The goal is to make every conversation and face-to-face interaction a meaningful conversation.

Try this process of planting, watering, and nourishing your conversations with your spouse, children, friends, business associates, and strangers in the marketplace. You should not be surprised at how much healthier your garden of relationships will grow with meaningful conversations.

Try this with your God. Plants some seeds, stop, wait, and listen for the watering of those seeds.

The Scriptures talk about loving the Lord your God with all your heart, with all your soul, with your entire mind, and with all your strength; and about loving your neighbor as yourself. That is one tall order!

For me, success with significance is an "all-in" approach to life in our relationships and our spiritual and emotional well-being. It is a no-holds-barred, taking on risk, being open, being vulnerable, and learning from rejection approach to living. In my mind, there is simply no other way to live. One could amass more than enough in terms of financial resources and have the physique and health of an Olympic athlete. But the greatest reward for living comes from investing your heart, mind, soul, and strength in those who cross our path on the roadway of refinement. You could say it starts with loving and taking care of me, so that I can love and take care of my neighbor or the people I interact with, so that I can honor my God and make Him proud!

ERM: As you assess your most important relationships, include planned, meaningful conversations that go far beyond the everyday news-weather-sports topics. Share why you value the relationship. Share your fears or concerns and areas you would like to improve upon. Ask what concerns them the most. Share stories of each other's funniest, scariest, or happiest moments. Share some of the significant emotionally, financially, and physically refining moments in your life and create some new ones together.

SECTION III

PHYSICAL REFINEMENT

CHAPTER 12

"IT'S OPENING NIGHT"

IF YOU WANT TO LOSE WEIGHT and improve your health, just browse the web, visit your local bookstore, or stay up and watch a late-night infomercial. There is a plethora of information and access to available resources. Visit your local health club and you will find the masses diligently working out, some for beauty and physique, some for camaraderie and a sense of belonging, some for beating back Mother Nature and the natural consequences of aging.

Let's face it, most people could stand to lose a few pounds, eat more grains and fruits and vegetables, and increase their level of exercise and activity. So why then do we as a population continue to go in the opposite direction or progress at a dismal rate in terms of our general health? Like most worthy and significant goals, the desired results can appear to be too far down the road, or unattainable—until you break them down into manageable daily routines and keep a constant focus on why you want to achieve the goal.

This section is not intended to compete with the latest health tip, fad diet, or exercise craze. The intention here is to lay a foundation, from perhaps a different perspective, as to why our physical health and physical appearance should matter.

Whether you like it or not, our physical appearance does make a difference. If you are 68 years old and are being considered for a position along with someone half your age, wouldn't you want to increase your odds? No matter what your age, others will form a first impression of you within seconds of meeting you. As it has been stated, "Life is a constant audition, and for every audience it is opening night."

If your objective is to live a life of continuous improvement, then your physical health needs to be a daily part of your refinement planning. Your ability to get up each morning, compete, and contribute is vitally important. In the spirit of continuous improvement, I will offer some practical, daily activities that will improve your health, improve your ability to compete, save you money, and improve your personal sense of worth.

Let's start with flossing. I hate flossing. It is but one small task that if I skip today, I will most likely skip again tomorrow. Does it really make a difference? Look at it from a different perspective. My smile is probably one of the first things people notice about me. I have invested time and effort into enhancing my smile—orthodontic work at the age of 32, regularly scheduled dental appointments, an electric toothbrush, etc. Your smile sets the stage for your daily interactions, and flossing is but one simple act that will make a difference.

> **Your smile sets the stage for your daily interactions.**

Flossing removes toxins from your mouth. These toxins lead to bad breath, gum disease, and other physical ailments, but just as important, this simple task is a daily reminder of your desire to seek and create physically refining moments. Daily flossing will ultimately save you in medical and dental expenses, it will increase your ability to compete in the workplace, and it will improve your self-esteem and confidence.

I don't expect you to suddenly enjoy flossing your teeth. But if you consider it from this perspective, you will forever welcome this discipline. As silly as it may sound, flossing becomes a daily FRM ritual and a daily reminder of what you want to accomplish in terms of your health and appearance. Flossing is a daily prayer for vitality.

GENERAL APPEARANCE

Business cards are almost becoming a thing of the past, but I will never forget my first business card. It clearly gave the receiver a sense of who I am, what I have accomplished, and what they can expect from me. Now think in terms of your general appearance. Your appearance is your primary business card—who you are, what you have accomplished, and what people can expect from you.

When I apply for a job, I feel so much more confident if I have taken the necessary steps for putting my best foot forward. My hair has been cut within a week, my nails are properly groomed, I have a close clean shave, I have a well-pressed shirt and matching tie, my shoes are shined, and even my car is freshly washed just because it makes me feel better and more confident. Considering that the days of staying with the same company for the next 30 years are gone, life really is, in a sense, a constant audition. I am all for kicking back, hanging out in shorts, T-shirts, or jeans when I am just staying home or close to town. But my general sense is to always put my best foot forward.

For some, this skill set comes quite naturally—you pay attention to your hairstyle, what's in fashion and appropriate for your age and line of work, etc. Others may want to consider seeking assistance from a friend or other resource such as a department store employee or a hairstylist. Here's a clue: if you've had the same hairstyle and general wardrobe for the past 20 years, you probably need some assistance, which is a polite way of saying "makeover" for us men.

Men, if you are growing those few strands of hair as long as they will possibly grow, you will actually appear younger and healthier if you go ahead and cut those strands back. If there are too few strands of hair to bother with, shave them off. A well-groomed man with a shaved head is considered athletic and cool.

If your eyeglasses, neckties, handbags, belts, and shoes haven't changed in the past 10 years or so, you probably need an upgrade. Consider these items to be the props on your personal stage of life.

Though you don't want to dress 20 or 30 years younger than your age, you should be somewhat contemporary and maintain a sense of style, even as you continue to age. There is something to be said about a more mature individual who carries him or herself well, head held high with a sense of style, be it casual or business attire. These people face each day with the expectation that something good is going to happen and that there will be refining moments too numerous to count.

Keep in mind that, since your general appearance is your personal business card, people will notice your general skin tone and complexion. Ladies, many of you are keenly aware of this and have already taken steps in the area of skin care. If it has been awhile, you might consider meeting with a representative from a department store cosmetic counter to make sure your makeup is up-to-date and appropriate for your personal style.

Men, for many of you, this is probably a newer concept. Gone are the days of washing your face with a bar of deodorant bath soap. Think in terms of living another 25 years past the traditional age of retirement. That face is the only one you have, so you'd better do all you can to protect it and keep it in tip-top shape, starting right now. Would you let your brand-new dream car sit outside, exposed to elements, and never wash, polish, or protect the outside finish? Of course not!

Your skin tone and appearance are general indications of your level of health and well-being. Are you worn out, stressed out, drinking too much alcohol, not getting enough sleep? Your face and complexion will tell the truth. What many men are not aware of is that with some basic daily steps of proper cleansing and using an SPF moisturizer (to protect against the harmful effects of the sun), you can improve your skin tone and reduce some of the visible lines of aging. You don't have to spend a lot of money on this.

If you are challenged by this idea, there are various skin care product lines for men. The packaging appears to be more masculine, but it's all basically the same stuff. You can start off with the basic products (for washing and moisturizing), or you seek the help of a skin care professional.

You are kidding yourself if you don't think your overall appearance and attractiveness will make a difference in the world of commerce. By attractive, I'm not referring to movie star good looks, and I'm certainly not referencing the area of romance. I am referring to a well-kept, organized, overall healthy appearance that "attracts" people to you. The more people you attract, the more you will interact; the more you interact, the more opportunities you will have for emotionally and financially refining moments.

The more people you attract, the more you will interact.

PRM: Attraction = Interaction = Refining Moments

CHAPTER 13

ROUTINE MEDICAL EXAMINATIONS

BACK TO THE ANALOGY OF owning a car. Why is it that many of us would never ignore an engine warning light or continue to drive our vehicle without ever changing the oil—but we can't think of the last time we had a complete physical examination? The same people who follow the prescribed service schedule for their cars have no clue which preventive and diagnostic procedures are warranted for their gender and age group.

Many of us take far better care of our automobile, our stock portfolio, or our career than our own general health. We may think, "I'll try and eat right, get some exercise from time to time, pop a vitamin or two, and if something breaks down, I'll go visit the doctor." But waiting for something to break down could be far too late. There is simply no excuse for not evaluating your overall heath and determining an action plan with the assistance of a doctor or qualified health practitioner.

> **Many of us take far better care of our automobile, our stock portfolio, or our career than our own general health.**

I am very serious about defining and writing out a plan of action. No business leader would accept your general thoughts of where you are and where you want to be this year with your business responsibilities; they want the plan spelled out, in writing, with specifics. Yet when it comes to our health, we're more vague about what needs to get checked out.

An appropriate call to action is to schedule your annual medical exam during your birth month. Think in terms of "Happy birthday to me!" When you arrive for your appointment, be prepared to discuss any changes from the previous year. Take a notepad with you and create a checklist of follow-up tests, recommended changes to diet, etc. That way, you can create an action plan of where you want to be in the next five to 10 years in terms of your physical health. This plan may even be worth sharing with someone who can help hold you accountable. Set an alert in your calendar to remind you of your important health tasks or milestones throughout the year.

CHIROPRACTIC CARE

A key resource for our overall health that is often overlooked, or only sought out once the damage is done, is chiropractors. My first encounter with a chiropractor was a result of the long-distance running I had done during my high school years. I was suffering from a severe case of shin splints and a knee injury. My primary care physician offered limited treatment options, so I sought out alternatives to traditional medicine. My observation is that there has been significant improvement in research and chiropractic treatment methodologies since the mid-1970s.

Unfortunately, our overweight, out-of-shape, sit-at-a-desk, stare-at-mobile-devices lifestyle is causing wear and tear on our bodies and throwing us out of alignment. If your desire is to maintain a high level of activity and save money in the long run, consider investing in chiropractic care. It can be a vital component to your preventive and comprehensive health regimen. Don't wait until you can't bend down to tie your own shoes. (My desire is to never be the speaker onstage wearing a business suit with Velcro tennis shoes.)

If you have any reason to suspect a change in your health, immediately schedule a follow-up appointment with your health practitioner. Do not delay or continue to procrastinate. We have but one physical body to get it right! Let's all put in place a smart action plan for health and vitality and commit to following through with it.

CHAPTER 14

NUTRITION

MANY OF US WILL AGREE that fast food can taste great! I am old enough to remember when McDonald's was still a fairly new concept. Its roots are in San Bernardino, California, the same city where I started my investment career. If you have ties to the West Coast, you are probably familiar with In-N-Out Burger, most likely one of the healthiest fast-food restaurants. Its original drive-through is located in Baldwin Park, California, the same city where my wife and I attended grammar school. To this day, In-N-Out Burger is usually our first stop when we fly into Los Angeles to visit our families.

Fast-food restaurants were created to meet the demands of the baby boomer generation. There were a lot of us kids, moms were starting to work outside the home, and often we found ourselves in a hurry. There were very few microwave ovens, and the benefits of the technology age—freeze-dried, flash frozen, etc.—were just around the corner. As a nation we were proud of our industrialized, manufacturing accomplishments, so why not embrace the same assembly line concept for food preparation? It was like magic. You walk up to the counter or speak into a speaker (or clown), place your order, and within minutes, "Your order is ready." That was fast!

When you are young, your body starts learning to adapt to the higher levels of sodium, simple carbohydrates, and sugar in fast foods—not a good thing, because your body starts to crave this cheaper source of body fuel and energy. As you age, your body becomes less tolerant of this cuisine. So while we may agree that fast food can taste great and is convenient when you are in a hurry, my first recommendation for a healthier diet is to simply slow down!

When you slow down, you will create a physically refining moment.

Slow down and think about your food as fuel.

Slow down and dedicate some time to planning what you will consume this week.

When you slow down, you will create a physically refining moment.

If we don't slow down and think in advance, we are more apt to fuel our bodies with an "inexpensive" drive-through experience. The true cost of that meal, though, is difficult to calculate as it will be reflected later in our expanding waistline (the need to purchase more clothes) and health care bills (as we pay the price for our declining health). The crash effect of coming off carbohydrates and sugar will affect our mood and energy level within a couple of hours—possibly causing you to snap at the kids when you arrive home for the evening. So did we really save that much time and money? The answer is no. We actually made an investment in a lower grade source of fuel.

By taking time to think in advance, we can plan a much healthier alternative, or a higher-grade level of fuel. For example, if you know you are going to have some drive time ahead or won't be eating for a while, you might pack some dry-roasted unsalted almonds and a bottle of water to help maintain your energy level and pacify your hunger. This good source of fuel will help buy you time before your next meal.

If you dig a little deeper into the reasons behind your fuel choices—beyond the motivations of time and expense—you may uncover even higher levels of motivation that will require you to take steps to reprioritize. Recognize that there are other competing motivations. Food can also represent a reward, comfort, social engagement, or culinary pleasure.

For me, food has always been a form of reward. I can remember my mom taking us kids out for a banana split to celebrate the last day of school, and while I'm not saying this was completely inappropriate, I do recognize that I can fall prey to deserving a reward for just about anything.

Completed an important project—I deserve a good meal.

Closed the big sale—I deserve a good meal.

Got a nice annual bonus—I deserve a good meal.

Survived a horrible workday—I deserve a good meal.

And, of course, TGIF—the whole family deserves a good meal!

So if I'm not going to ignore my desire for a celebratory meal, I must redefine what a good meal is. I have come to appreciate that "good" can be defined as

- Home-cooked: Slower cooked versus instant processed food items and cooked with a mixture of spices instead of too much salt.
- Having variety: Different vegetables; proteins such as fish, lean meats, chicken, soy, and tofu.
- Made with whole grains: Breads, cereals, and other sources of fiber.
- Hydrating: Water, red wine, and black coffee (the latter two in moderation). One glass of wine and a "half-caff" (blend of regular and decaffeinated coffee) are examples of moderation. If carbonated or sugared drinks are a part of your diet, do a little more research to determine how many you can afford per week. Discovering different teas

can be quite interesting and beneficial to your overall health.
- Portion-controlled: Unless you are a farmer working 12 hours a day in the field, you cannot afford to eat a "farmers breakfast." Eat slower, and your smaller portions will do just fine.

If you are going to have a serving of "comfort food" or dessert, plan in advance and make a note in your calendar to assist you in limiting the frequency of this type of fuel.

My newly discovered priority for my daily diet is to ingest an efficient, quality fuel source. And to slow down and savor it. The great news is that by giving thought to the foods I choose and to planning, I can easily minimize my expense and maximize the taste and the social pleasure I associate with a good meal.

Slow down, plan, and then stop—stop eating at least two hours before going to bed. Give your digestive system a break and you will get a better night of sleep.

CHAPTER 15

EXERCISE

WHEN I WAS A YOUNG CHILD in the 1960s, we would play hard and sleep hard. It seems we were always outside playing.

Many fathers, like mine, earned a living doing work that involved physical labor. (I am amazed at how fatigued I can be after eight hours of working at a desk, burning very few calories throughout the day.) As a child, we had no gardener. It was me who powered our mower, and we all dug dirt, pulled weeds, and hauled out the garbage. Household chores were no easier—mopping, dusting, pushing a heavy vacuum cleaner, sometimes scrubbing while on our knees, hanging laundry out to dry. I am sure we kids probably complained, but truth be told, we enjoyed the camaraderie and the sense of fulfillment that accompanied a job well done. Our chores were nothing compared to my father's—he grew up on a farm—and he would often tell us, "You've got it easy!" (I can't even fathom my father's response if I ever asked him, "So Dad, what do you think you will do for exercise today? Badminton, perhaps?")

In the days past, we rarely had to give conscious thought to exercise. But I was a child during the transition from the industrial age to the information age. The comforts of modernization were slowing us down. I can recall my mother placing a chair in the living room, getting her exercise stretch band out of the closet, and adjusting the black-and-white television set as she prepared to exercise with Jack LaLanne. I would sometimes join her in her stretching moves as Jack would tell us to raise our arms and take a deep breath in, as the music of an old organ would climb up the scale—"Hold it, hold it, hold it, arms back down and breathe out" (and the music would slide back down). LaLanne was a pioneer of television fitness and exercise. He was the only option for stay-at-home mothers wishing to improve their health and appearance. (And remember, there were no VCRs to record the show for viewing at a more convenient time.)

Fast-forward to today and there's no shortage of health (social) clubs, exercise gyms, yoga and Pilates studios, extreme sports, boot camp DVDs, kickboxing, personal trainers, and children's exercise video games. It seems like we have to find an expensive proposition in order to accomplish a day's worth of sufficient exercise.

Don't get me wrong—I've tried and enjoyed most of the above. And I strongly encourage you to find a healthy hobby, something you enjoy, be it bicycling or power yoga. With our sedentary lifestyle, we could all use an extra boost. But the point I want to make is to not wait for the "right" exercise program to come along before deciding to exercise.

If you can work it into your budget, my suggestion is to hire a personal trainer to assess your overall physical abilities and to augment or create an appropriate exercise routine. I credit our trainer, Kimberly, with giving us a new lease on life when we needed it the most. The inspiration she provided and the formulation of an exercise plan that required no expensive or elaborate exercise equipment was extremely beneficial. There were many mornings when Becky and I would grudgingly head down to the basement to work out, only because we knew Kimberly was going to arrive on Saturday morning and it would be obvious to her if we skipped our routine.

In addition, Becky became a volunteer firefighter in her late forties, and there is no way she would have survived the rigors of the academy without Kimberly's assistance. I believe working out with her proved to be a significant refining moment for Becky as she was encouraged with her increased physical strength and stamina. Becky was motivated to push herself beyond any perceived limitations or expectations of what a "middle-age" woman could do. We are both forever grateful to Kimberly for her expertise in the field of diet and exercise.

But again, don't wait for the right trainer or exercise program to come along. Develop and commit to a conscious effort of exercise throughout your day, each and every day, up until your very last breath.

When you contemplate the fundamentals of exercise, physical movement, or action, the commitment becomes so much more reasonable and easier to adopt for a lifetime.

- Cardiorespiratory: a fancy term for heartbeat and breathing. This means if you are reading this, your heart is beating and you are breathing. You're off to a good start! With more movement or action, you will increase your heart rate and breaths per minute. Have you consciously increased your heart or breathing rate today? (Stress and fear do not count.) On your list could be walking at a faster pace, taking the stairs, parking the car at a greater distance, doing calf raises or squats while in your office, walking the mall, walking around your office during your lunch break, or playing with your kids or grandchildren.

> **Have you consciously increased your heart or breathing rate today?**

- Stretching and strengthening: building muscle tissue by stretching and relaxing a muscle group. Make a tight fist and hold it for five seconds, then open your fist and relax. If you repeated that same motion over and over again, you would develop a stronger group of hand and arm muscles. What are the benefits of stretched and strengthened muscle groups? They're too numerous to list completely but include:
    - Support to your vital organs
    - Prevention of disease, from the increased removal of toxins from your body
    - More efficient burning of calories
    - Support to your posture and balance, which prevents you from falling
    - If you do fall, a much greater chance of avoiding injury
    - Improved general appearance
- Other strengthening: carrying your bags, groceries, kids, and pets. Try push-ups, leg squats, calf raises, leg raises, modified sit-ups, exercise bands, small free weights for arms curls, and stretching moves.
- Balance and posture: It turns out Mom was right about standing straight and not slouching. First of all, standing and sitting with your back straight and your head properly aligned gives you a more

credible, confident appearance; but there are also short-term and long-term health benefits. When you are going about your day, you will be less prone to neck muscle fatigue, strain on your back, and headaches. As you continue to age, a proper posture and balance can literally be a matter of life and death. The number of seniors who die after a fall, broken hip, injury, or infection could be drastically reduced with education and proper exercise.

PRM: Start today by raising up one leg and slowly squatting down and raising yourself back up. Have a chair or some other form of support nearby as you do this exercise. Consult with a personal trainer for additional core strength and balancing exercises. Make this physically refining moment a daily priority.

CHAPTER 16

REST AND RECOVERY

ALL IS FOR NAUGHT WITHOUT a proper night's sleep. Certainly you can lead a fairly healthy life and enjoy financial success and the company of friends without a good amount of sleep, but it won't be as easy. More importantly, why sell yourself short from your full potential? Are there potentially refining moments that you are just too fatigued to recognize and respond to?

Trust me, I speak from experience. I know what it is like to work the graveyard shift and never quite catch up on sleep. The first and the last shifts of your workweek can be the worst because you don't want to miss out on seeing the sunshine—so you sleep a few hours and then force your body to pretend you had a full

We seem to take pride in charging ahead with a lack of sleep.

night's rest. For some odd reason, as a society we seem to take pride in charging ahead with a lack of sleep.

You might get a nice rush of adrenaline when you have a busy schedule, are working hard on a project and making money, or are thinking of a big upcoming vacation—a habit similar to cramming for a test while in school. You love the challenge, and the upcoming deadline motivates you into overdrive.

Or you might have too much going on, and the stresses of life are piling up. You know you need to sleep, but your mind won't shut off, so you lay there, drifting in and out of sleep, later waking up knowing you never really rested.

The problem with these scenarios is that you can get by for some time with them, but as you age, your mind and body will become less resilient to an inadequate amount of sleep. Your vital organs are feeling the impact. There can be a psychological toll, and not unlike other unhealthy habits, you may not notice the negative effects until years later when it is much harder to recover.

If you have no choice but to forgo a good night's sleep—dealing with sick kids, working two jobs to put food on the table (been there, done that)—can we at least agree you need to optimize your sleep time so you are truly resting?

> **Rest:** a state or period of refreshing freedom.

Understand the definitions of rest, which include: a state or period of refreshing freedom from exertion; the repose of sleep that is refreshing to body and mind and is marked by a reduction in metabolic activity; and freedom from mental or emotional anxiety.

Read that again, slowly, and savor each and every word. Refreshing, isn't it?

PRM: There is a significant difference between sleep and rest, and the truth is, you need both.

Toward the latter part of my respiratory therapy career, I began to develop an interest in sleep studies, and I participated in the developmental stages of a sleep laboratory for our hospital. I know for certain the sophistication of these sleep labs has grown over the years, but at that time, we would bring in a patient and measure various vital signs such as heart rhythm and oxygen levels as the patient drifted off to sleep. The intent was to have the patient reach a deep enough level of sleep in order to determine if the person experienced episodes of sleep apnea, a disorder characterized by abnormal pauses in breathing or instances of abnormally low breathing during sleep. The medical literature at the time presented information where some people could literally drop their head and fall asleep during the middle of a conversation because their body was so deprived of rest and recovery. Their body was never fully resting or recharging for the next day. Their body was being deprived of oxygen each night, and the vital organs were struggling for survival. Their health was failing to a point of critical consequence.

While sleep apnea poses immediate risks that many of us will, hopefully, never encounter, if we are not truly resting in our sleep, there is a risk to our physical and mental well-being.

Truly resting in your sleep means getting to a point where, metabolically and emotionally, your body is recovering from the physical and emotional stresses of the day.

What steps can we take to fully benefit from the daily refining moment of sleep and relaxation? For many, it may simply require a reprioritization of daily routines:

- Recognize the absolute importance of sleep (7 to 9 hours per night is a good average). Consider it another daily chore and the body's reward for a job well done.
- Cut back on your daily caffeine intake.
- Stop eating two hours before going to bed.
- Invest in a quality mattress, pillow, and bedding.
- Make sure your room is dark.
- Cut back on television, Internet, or aggressive music before going to bed ("breaking news" is meant to excite you, not relax you).
- Develop a slowing-down ritual as you prepare for sleep. Do not just jump into bed and close your eyes; you might sleep but won't truly rest.

- Write down any pressing priorities for the next day, then lay the list aside.
- Take slow deep breaths, constrict and relax each arm and leg, and note the positive effects of relaxation.
- Pray and/or meditate on your blessings of the day; pray and meditate on behalf of others who are experiencing emotional, financial, or physical needs; pray and meditate for wisdom to recognize and purposefully respond to the refining moments of the next day to come.

Physical strength, energy, and stamina are vital components to a life of personal refinement. Improved physical health increases our ability to contribute to others and to society as a whole. Our physical appearance can be a barometer of our general health and a conduit for increasing personal interactions, leading to increased opportunities for significant refining moments. Our ability to recharge our mind, body, and soul inspires us to greet the new day with determination, joy, perseverance, confidence, and optimism.

SECTION IV

FINANCIAL REFINEMENT

CHAPTER 17

WHERE ARE WE? WHERE ARE WE GOING?

IT IS AMAZING TO ME, even with 25 years under my belt in this industry, how complex the financial world has become. The previous decade proved that many of the so-called experts really had no idea what they were talking about—tech bubbles, housing bubbles, good old-fashioned greed ... Legendary investor Warren Buffet once commented, "In MBA school, they should hand out the assignment of valuating a tech company, and anyone that turns in a paper should get an F."

Consider the following financial equation:

Politics + Complex Financial Markets
= Financial Crisis

There are many, more qualified authors who could provide an exhaustive analysis of the near collapse of our financial markets and the bursting of the housing bubble.

But it's safe to say that much of the crisis can be traced to ignorance and greed.

Unfortunately, the Pareto principle, or the 80-20 rule, applies to the state of our American population and their prospects for a traditional retirement. It has been reported that 80 percent of the American population is not saving enough to be on track for retirement at age 65. Whether you are in the 20 percent or the 80 percent group, let me offer a practical, no-nonsense approach to getting ahead financially.

- Know where you are and where you are going.
- Avoid the urge to splurge.
- Protect, save, and invest.

That's it! It turns out your grandparents and great-grandparents knew what they were talking about. It sounds so simple, but the number of households actually sticking to this basic approach is drastically low.

In the earliest days of my investment career, I was told to have a stock recommendation ready to go at all times—a "cocktail napkin" presentation. The thinking was, if someone came up to you at a party and asked what you did for a living, once you responded, you would be asked if you had a hot stock tip and you should immediately follow-up with an investment idea. What I learned over the years is that many people have no business investing.

Hear me out.

My employment income has always been related to "money in motion," or the need for people to invest. Investing in the U.S. and global economies is fundamental to our capitalist society, and I strongly favor the opportunities that investing for our financial future affords us. The problem is, many of us fail to fully appreciate just how important it is to have a strong foundation before we invest our hard-earned dollars. I believe our 24/7 world of information and communication has fueled our speculative appetite. Sadly, many of our financial decisions are fueled by either fear or greed and the current news hype of today. We may not know what to do, but we feel we should do something or else we will fall behind. In addition, many of us have a naturally competitive nature, and if our friend is bragging about today's return on their stock or investment pick, we assume they must be doing something right and, therefore, we are doing something wrong.

> **Sadly, many of our financial decisions are fueled by either fear or greed and the current news hype of today.**

A reminder before we continue: Financial success is the ability to live in a manner in which you are accustomed, whether or not you choose to work.

By this definition, I have known some very *successful* people—house, cars, trips, clothes, luxury items—and while their income has been far from federal standards for the definition of poverty, if that income suddenly stopped (due to the loss of a job or retirement), they could not continue with their lifestyle.

About 10 years ago, I created a training program for my employer entitled "Financial Success and Your 401(k)." I would travel the country holding educational meetings for the company's employees and, admittedly, it was a boost to my ego when someone would approach me after the meeting to ask some questions or seek my advice. Following one workshop, a middle-age gentleman approached and asked if he could share something with me. He appeared to be in some sort of technical or operational type of position: casually dressed, access card around his neck, just an average Joe. Of course I said yes.

What came next was an ERM humbling experience! A refining moment at its finest. This employee showed me his brokerage statement and proceeded in a very humble manner. "I've been doing everything you have talked about all along." He lived within his means, he had a strong financial foundation, his goals were well defined, and he followed a basic prudent man's investment approach. He would easily have the ability to live in a manner in which he was accustomed, whether or not he chose to work! Truth be known, it should have been him flying around the country teaching those workshops. He had attained financial success. He actually practiced what I was preaching.

Let's take a closer look (below and into the next chapter) at the bullet points previously shared.

Know where you are and where you are going.

The first step toward financial well-being is to have a budget. As I have shared with my workshop attendees on countless occasions, I have always had a budget … and just like my diet, on Monday I plan to get back on track. With a budget, like any business (not our government), you will enter how much money is coming into your household and how much money you plan to spend. The added bonus is knowing precisely where your money has been spent. I dare you—no, I double-dog dare you—to track every single dime you spend for 30 days. If you complete this mission, you will be surprised to learn just how much money you are capable of spending without even knowing it.

I know once I get a $20 bill in my pocket and then break it down, it's gone! Case in point: I'm heading to the airport and need some cash, so I stop by the ATM and get $20. At the airport, I pass through security and now I need a bottled water and maybe a fresh cup of coffee. Oh, I should get a newspaper to read on the plane. Wait, what is SHE doing on the cover of *People* magazine? I have to buy a copy—for my wife, of course.

Most of us have no idea just how much we spend per day, per month, or per year.

You get the picture. I venture to say that most of us have no idea just how much we spend per day, per month, or per year. And unfortunately, we are passing the same bad habit on to our children.

Can a latte a day keep the budget astray? If you budget for it, great! Just know that $5 per day in unaccounted miscellaneous spending adds up to $1,825 a year. If you deposited that $1,825 every year for the next 30 years, at 7 percent interest you could expect almost $200,000. Now that's a "latte" money!

My mom and dad still have their first budget book from their earliest years of marriage. This is long before the days of calculators, computer programs, and ATM machines. This book contained a simple handwritten ledger of what money was coming in and what amount was going out. In the book were some envelopes; one was labeled "food," another "mortgage." The theory being, on payday Dad cashed his check—yes, he actually stood in line and walked out with cash—and placed the cash allotments in the appropriate envelopes. When they spent the money from the envelope, guess what? They were done. That was it!

Can you imagine how much better off we would all be (governments included) if we maintained this good old-fashioned discipline? So please, don't even talk to me about your hot investment idea if you are not following this basic first step.

FRM: Track every expense for 30 days.

A budget will help you know where you are now so you can know how to aim for where you want to be in the future. Most of us are used to thinking in terms of a one- or five-year plan for our careers; but what about our thoughts in terms of money? Bill Bacharach—a noted author, trainer, and speaker for advisors in the financial world—shares a simple question that can have a profound impact on your goal-planning process: "What's important about money to you?" Take time to really work through this question.

Ask yourself other peripheral questions like:

What's important about having choices?

Maybe the answer is, "I don't want to be stuck in some dead-end job and be forced to live where I don't want to live."

What's important about not being stuck in a dead-end job?

Maybe it's, "I feel like I have been given much in terms of talent, ability to learn, and motivation. I want to contribute more to society, and I feel I deserve to be well compensated for my efforts. This brings me deep-rooted personal satisfaction, and I find much joy in providing for my loved ones."

Once you dig deep and work through this self-evaluation of what really motivates you in terms of money, you are on the right path to better defining your financial goals above and beyond just making more money or getting a higher interest rate. Why attempt to follow a disciplined budget and savings plan? Why attempt to follow a smart investment plan? Heck, why should I get up in the morning and go to work?

In working with countless individuals over the years and attempting to assist them in determining their highest motivating factor for investing their funds, the conversation becomes far more than, "Well, I just want a higher rate!" When you start to drill down, watch out! I have heard emotionally charged comments such as, "Well, I remember my aunt having to go from house to house in her final years, with various families having to take care of her, and I don't want that happening to me! I don't want to be a burden to anyone."

Now there's a very strong, compelling understanding of where someone is and where that person wants to be. We have emotionally defined a goal worth taking the time and effort to achieve.

Understand that every goal you set may not be quite so significant, but the point is to drill down to the emotional level (ERM + FRM) as to why you have a certain goal and why this goal is worthy of being accomplished. Only then will you be on the right path with the odds of success in your favor.

Some examples of worthy goals and reasons for them:
- Saving for your child's college education.

Why? My father never had an opportunity to complete his education. I advanced, but my options were limited. I want my son to have a choice, in fact, many choices. By completing his formal education, he will have an opportunity to pursue his highest calling and aspiration. His world will be filled with numerous prospects for growth. His prospects for societal impact will only be limited by his desire to dream and put forth effort.

Now there's a reason to save and invest.

- Save for a down payment on a house.

Why? Because it is expected? Not good enough. How about the freedom to stay in one location if we want to stay; and the ability to establish roots within a community, to take time to learn more about our children's schools, and to contribute to the well-being of our neighborhood.

FRM: Write down your financial goals or take a second look at goals you have previously set and ask yourself, "What's important about that goal to me?" Drill down, repeating the question at least five times per goal. A financial goal (FRM) validated with a deep emotional purpose (ERM) has a significantly increased chance of survival and accomplishment.

A financial goal (FRM) validated with a deep emotional purpose (ERM) has a significantly increased chance of survival and accomplishment.

CHAPTER 18

FINANCIAL PLANNING FUNDAMENTALS

BACK TO THE BULLET POINTS from the previous chapter: *Avoid the urge to splurge.*

Okay, now I really feel like a hypocrite. But I know from experience what I am talking about, and I have plenty of friends and neighbors who have the same issues: Why do we buy things that we don't need to impress people we don't really like?

My urge to splurge is not my fault because I have been targeted by marketers my entire life. I grew up with the modern age of television commercials and marketing campaigns looking for their next "consumption recruit." And I must admit, with the right jingle and visual images, I can be persuaded to buy just about anything.

It doesn't take a licensed psychologist to know that much of our FRMs—such as buying new clothes, upgrading our technological gadgets, and buying a new car—are directly tied to our ERMs, our deep-rooted psyche (who we are) or our perception of what we would like to be:

> You are not good looking enough.
> Your car is making the wrong statement about what you've become.
> Your clothes are so last winter.
> Your hair is the wrong color.
> Your cell phone isn't keeping up.
> Your kids are deprived.
> That coffee tastes good but not great!
> This could save you more time.
> You can attract more friends.
> You need to keep up, keep up, keep up.

Imagine if just one day, you turned on the television or radio and every commercial break sounded something like this: "Today is a great day, so count your blessings, be grateful for what you have, and call someone just to let them know that you were thinking of them."

Or this: "Life is good, and I have all that I really need."

Now, don't get me wrong—I am a capitalist and an optimist at heart. I work hard to increase my purchasing power, but in our world of easy credit (buy now, pay later), I am afraid many of us have drifted far off course in determining what we really need and making purchases only when we have truly saved up enough money.

Case in point, the housing bubble that suddenly popped. Years ago, you worked hard, saved, saved, and saved to buy a home. For most, the home represented the fruits of your labor and security for your family. Paying off the mortgage was considered a key pillar in your financial plan for retirement. Fast-forward to our modern era. For many, the home has become a key source of prestige and something that you can easily finance, flip for a profit, or walk away from if it doesn't work out. It has become disposable, like many of our other status symbols and goods we purchase.

One or two generations ago, many people did not have what we might consider much "wealth," but it is amazing how much was saved, fixed, or created using items most of us would consider trash today. As a child, I can recall seeing an odd but creative jewelry holder sitting on top of my grandmother's dresser. The jewelry holder was nothing more than a countertop Tic-Tac mint display holder, but you know what? It worked. My grandmother, an eco-friendly recycler. Who knew?

I am all about quality, craftsmanship, living in the best neighborhood, and driving the safest car that I can afford. The problem is, without much thought, I could easily talk myself into buying just about anything.

ERM: Ask yourself, at least five times, do I really need to make this purchase?

PROTECT, SAVE, AND INVEST

By now you may be wondering, "I thought you were an investment guy. Where's my hot investment recommendation?" Trust me, hot recommendations come and go. My experience is that true creation of wealth and financial security is achieved by covering the basics first. There is a time and a place for speculation, and a speculative investment in real estate, business ventures, or equity (stock) markets can certainly reward you for your effort. But if you are not taking care of some basic financial principles first, you are no better off than simply buying a lottery ticket. And, as a former pastor of mine, Tom Mercer, stated years ago, "The lottery is nothing more than a tax on the mathematically challenged."

The first financial investment you should make is in yourself—more specifically, in your ability to think, contribute, and earn.

PROTECT

The first financial investment you should make is in yourself—more specifically, in your ability to think, contribute, and earn. How? Invest in yourself through a monthly contribution into a basic life insurance policy, and don't rely on the one you pick up from your employer. There is no excuse not to have one; you would be hard-pressed to find me someone who has absolutely no one depending on them financially in some way.

You could be a well-compensated, educated individual with ideas that will pay off in the future. But if you don't wake up one day, it really doesn't matter, does it? If you have a spouse or a partner, or if you have minor or elderly dependents, you must ensure that they will have the financial ability to continue their life, as they know it, without you or your income. It's that simple.

TERM INSURANCE VERSUS PERMANENT INSURANCE

The insurance industry, products, and services have evolved dramatically over the past several years. Associated costs have gone down. If you have a policy issued before 2000, you are past due for a policy review. From a very basic standpoint, it is much like renting versus purchasing a home. If I cannot afford the home I would like, then I am going to rent the nicest home, in the safest neighborhood and with the best schools, that I can afford. Term insurance allows you to rent, for a much smaller dollar amount, an adequate amount of coverage to replace your income. In the event of your death, the money transfers tax free and without probate to your named beneficiaries.

If you can budget for some tax-deferred growth, then you might consider shopping for a permanent policy (whole or universal life) that combines life coverage with investment funds.

I believe there are some ERM and FRM ramifications for both options (term and whole life) as well:

FRM: I want to maintain my health to the best of my ability because it lowers my cost of insurance.

ERM: I know with confidence, that as I commute, exercise, and go about my daily routine, if I am no longer here, my loved ones will be able to continue living in a manner, in which they have become accustomed, and this gives me some comfort in a world filled with stress and uncertainty.

FRM: If it has been more than five years since your life insurance was reviewed, get your policy reviewed by a trusted financial professional.

SAVE

Early in my investment career, I became fond of the phrase "Cash is trash," meaning today is a perfect time to invest. While I do believe that staying invested at all times, through various economic cycles, is imperative to long-term financial success, I've since learned that a certain amount of cash is crucial. Here again, the older generation was right: you should have three to six months of income stashed away in a savings account (or cash equivalents). With the last recession, many have learned that upward to a year or more is even more desirable.

REFINING MOMENTS | 163

So what is cash? Cash is money that you can easily access within one year or less—for example, a six-month certificate of deposit (CD) with a bank or a liquid money market account.

The pro to holding on to cash: there is little or no risk to your principal, meaning what you put in is what you can take out.

The con: what you put in is effectively all you will take out, meaning there really is no growth on your account. Yes, you can shop around for a higher short-term rate on your savings or CD, but when you consider the effects of inflation, you are lucky if you break even with the interest you've earned.

The main purpose is to have an emergency fund for unexpected needs or a temporary loss of income. Contrary to popular belief, and I stand guilty as charged, your home equity line of credit and 401(k) are not piggy banks.

Having spent most of my life in the Golden State, I figured we could always recover from a temporary financial setback because our house was always going up in value and the next credit card invitation was in today's mail. For far too many of us, the lessons learned from being cut off from these sources of funds have been quite difficult, and the ramifications may last for years.

FRM: Commit to an automatic payroll deduction directly into an interest-bearing savings account and consider selling off one of your "toys" to jump-start the balance.

INVEST

Alas, we are finally at the point where many people want to start first: the world of investments, money in motion, capitalism, sometimes greed, and Wall Street.

Before we talk about Wall Street, let's take a refresher on why we invest. The main purpose of investing is to surpass inflation. Simply put, inflation means that there is a good chance you will pay more for goods and services in the future. If 30 years ago, your grandmother hid $10,000 under the mattress so she could buy a new car, she would be surprised to find out her money will only buy an adequate used car in today's market—and forget about buying gas! Prices went up, but her initial dollar amount did not. However, if I invest my money, I need to earn enough to cover the cost of inflation and the taxes that will be owed on interest, dividends, and capital gains. In a nutshell, this is the basic rationale for investing.

So what is Wall Street? It is an actual street located in lower Manhattan, New York, and is the home to probably our greatest example of a free-market society. In 1792, a group of 24 "stockbrokers" met underneath a buttonwood tree and founded the New York Stock Exchange.

In 1986, as a rookie financial consultant with Merrill Lynch, I had the opportunity to visit the floor of the exchange. There is so much more to our global economy than the exchange, and much business takes place away from it, but here is where the exchange of capital (money) for ownership in a company (opportunity) happens. A stock exchange is literally an auction: how much are you willing to pay me in exchange for a certificate of ownership (fractional share) of a particular company? While the financial world has changed dramatically over the years with various financial instruments, financially engineered products, hedge funds, etc., I feel it is important to recollect the basics of investing before proceeding. If we can fully appreciate the basics, we may have a better opportunity to stay the course and invest with certainty of purpose.

Even if you consider yourself a seasoned investor, stay with me because I am afraid far too many of us have drifted off a course of reason. Let's back up even a step or two before this auction takes place under the buttonwood. The refresher will serve well in reminding us of what has made our nation so great: with hard work and good effort, anyone can have an opportunity to succeed!

If we can fully appreciate the basics, we may have a better opportunity to stay the course and invest with certainty of purpose.

STOCKS AND BONDS

If I were to start a business, I would gather whatever funds I could muster and start selling my product. For this example, let's call it Karl's Katering. Let's say with my savings account and the sale of a few assets, I come up with enough cash to purchase the necessities for cooking, serving, and delivering food for groups of up to 100. Within a year, word of mouth and local advertising have brought me good fortune. Friends and associates are encouraging me to expand. The problem if I expand is the need for another delivery truck, an upgraded kitchen, more storage space, and some formal advertising. I feel in my heart of hearts that I can be successful, but I don't have any available cash on hand.

Well then, let's head out to the buttonwood (before the days of social networking) and see if I can find someone to exchange some cash for an interest in my great company.

BONDS

The first level of cash is a loan, an IOU. This is known as a debt instrument or a bond. It is a note that states, if you loan me money, I will pay your money back at a certain date in the future, and while you are waiting for your money back, I will pay you interest on the loan.

If I am a new business owner with a limited track record and limited financial resources, you should expect a higher interest rate from me than you would be compensated from a bank. Basically, I am a "junk bond." Think about it: no bank would lend money at the same rate to every single customer. A bank is going to loan at a more favorable rate to a well-qualified borrower and at a much higher interest rate to someone with a few bankruptcies on his record. Likewise, a financially strong company can borrow money at a much lower rate than a company that's in financial trouble.

For my hypothetical company, I borrow the money to expand by offering bonds. I then buy what is needed for growth, and my business starts booming. In fact, I have been fortunate enough to be featured on a local newscast highlighting my continued success. I am Colorado's Small Business of the Year.

One of the bondholders gives me a call and says, "You know that $10,000 I loaned you and you planned to pay back at the end of 10 years? Well, I heard you have done quite well so I want to be paid back even more." Is the bondholder entitled to any more money? The answer is, "No. You loaned me money and I have promised to pay you back. That's it." The advantage to the bondholder is if the opposite happens, the company starts to collapse, the bondholder is one of the first in line to collect repayment from any assets sold off during liquidation.

The bondholder's attitude is, "If you do well, I want to do well." The answer, then, is, "Well, the great news is I am now going to offer stock in my company."

STOCKS

Stock is nothing more than taking an equity stake or a piece of ownership in a company. The number of shares, multiplied by the current share price, values the company. If a company continues to grow its revenue and profits, the expectation is my fractional ownership will be worth more than I paid should I decide to cash out. If the company does well, I will do well. Likewise, if the company fails, I will have to stand in line behind every bondholder waiting to collect. If there is any money left, I will be paid something, but more than likely if the company has truly failed, there will be nothing left and my certificate of ownership will be worthless.

This is what took place under the buttonwood tree on Wall Street so many years ago. Money exchanged hands for buying and selling stocks and bonds. You did not have to be born a king or a queen: the kid shining shoes on the street corner could save up and his money was just as good as anyone else's. You could walk up under that tree and say, "Let me buy a piece of the American dream!"

I've purposely drilled down the basics of investing because I believe there is a tremendous opportunity for all of us to participate. The problem is that some are so frightened they choose not to invest, and some are so greedy they attempt to manipulate their investments to a point of no return.

So now that you have a basic understanding of stocks and bonds, let's break down the general characteristics even further.

For stocks:
- Small capitalization (generally companies with market capitalization of between $300 million and $2 billion)
- Mid cap
- Large cap
- Growth
- Value
- Domestic or international (global)

For bonds:
- High quality or lower quality
- Shorter term or longer term
- Issued by corporate, government, or state municipalities

ASSET ALLOCATION

These various stocks and bonds can work together to create a specifically tailored recipe, or "allocation," that greatly increases your odds of achieving your investment goal within your time frame and within your comfort level, or risk-tolerance.

Just like in restaurants, there is a basic recipe that is created with known ingredients. The ingredients within an investment portfolio are listed above. If you like your food a bit spicier, you might add some hot sauce or chili powder. For investments, "spicier" means you can accept more risk for the prospect of earning a higher rate of return, so you might increase your allocation toward lower quality bonds, smaller companies, or international stocks. At one point, Apple and Microsoft were considered small-cap stocks whose long-term prospects were unknown. So when you buy a small stock, are you buying the next Pets.com (which went bankrupt during the dot-com bubble) or are you buying the next Microsoft?

As you age, spicier foods may not be the best thing for you. Likewise, in your investment portfolio, as you age, you might back off some of the spicier investment categories and allocate more toward larger, well-known, proven companies and higher-rated corporate bonds. The large proven company will not double in size or sales overnight, but you don't expect them to fail overnight either.

No two individuals are exactly alike, and no two investment portfolios should be exactly the same. If your investment assets are less than $250,000, you could be well served with some mutual funds that are closely aligned with your desired and needed investment objective. Think in terms of an already prepared, ready-to-go, heat-and-serve meal.

As your assets grow to more significant levels, you might be better served with your own, custom-designed asset allocation, tailored to your specific needs and goals. However you choose to seek advice, keep in mind that you should be managing the downside (risk) just as aggressively as you are managing the upside (potential gains). I strongly encourage you to shop around and ask for recommendations for an investment professional who will listen, explain, and communicate a disciplined investment program. If this person cannot do that, then move on and find someone else who can.

Obviously, I have simplified what can be a very complex, intellectual subject. This book is not intended to give specific investment advice. My purpose here is to bring you back to a foundation of common sense and reason. One recommendation I can make with certainty is that you need to view the world of investing from a learning orientation versus a performance orientation. Learn more about your emotional connections to money and what really matters most to you in terms of your immediate, intermediate, and longer-term goals. Learn more about general investment vehicles. Learn more about the companies and representatives you are considering to work alongside you.

Learn more about your emotional connections to money and what really matters most to you in terms of your immediate, intermediate, and longer-term goals.

FRM: Once you are ready to invest, think in terms of fine cuisine. Create a gourmet meal prepared to your liking. Do not settle for financial junk food!

SECTION V

PROFILES OF REFINEMENT

From a practical perspective, what does a life of refinement look like? The following pages profile three individuals who have recognized and capitalized on key refining moments in their personal and professional lives. They are not being highlighted here as "superstars," for I am sure each one would admit to continued and additional growth opportunities. And that's the point! There are no superstars. If there were, then you and I might as well pack up and exit the path of continuous improvement. Every one of us has room for growth. Our own unique successes and setbacks prepare us for our unique purpose and expand our potential to positively impact those we come into contact with on a financial, physical, and emotional level.

> **Every one of us has room for growth.**

The three individuals here exemplify significant progress in all three areas of refinement. My life has been enriched and refined by crossing paths with them.

CHAPTER 19

A NEW MILLENNIUM: VIOLET IGOLNIKOV

THERE WE WERE, THE YEAR 2000, and I was still trying to comprehend why I had not gotten to the next rung on the corporate ladder that I was climbing at Bank of America. Why was I now employed with a much smaller investment firm? The pace was so much slower, and the income levels of the financial consultants here were much lower, too. I found myself questioning my career with a "poor me, why am I here?" attitude.

It's at times like these that we need to be open to our next refining moment.

Enter Violet Igolnikov, who represented the up-and-coming generation of corporate professionals at this smaller firm and who, several years later, commented on how our first meeting and our work association dramatically changed her life. She has forever positively impacted my life as well.

I was conducting interviews for an open position in Orange County, one of the most competitive locations in Southern California, a job that can make or break the brightest of financial professionals.

At the very first sight of Violet, I could tell she was energetic and vibrant. I had just parked my car at a local branch office and spotted her confidently walking across the parking lot into the office to meet with me for a job interview. This young lady demonstrated a level of passion and energy that proved to be quite refreshing during our first meeting. Violet came across as a dynamic communicator as she relayed to me the various refining moments in her life and short career up to this point. Of course, she was not thinking specifically in terms of refining moments, but that is exactly what she accomplished during our first meeting. She seemed to be able to connect with my natural thought process as we easily exchanged information.

Violet didn't profess to be the smartest, brightest, or most experienced individual; admittedly, her resume was somewhat lean. She resigned from Merrill Lynch, with only six months on the job, after the dot-com tech bubble burst. But she didn't hesitate as she presented me with numerous reasons why she should be my number one candidate for the position. She did a great job, and I was convinced—she was my number two pick for the position.

The number one candidate was a gentleman who was very polished, presented himself well, and had a far more impressive resume, which included an MBA. But for some reason, neither the direct hiring manager nor I were able to reach this candidate. We wanted to make him an offer, but he didn't return our phone calls, and I needed to fill this position as soon as possible.

So now I am face-to-face with Violet, and as I begin to extend her an offer, my cell phone rings. I take the call only because it is the other hiring manager and I need to be certain there is no last-minute detail before I finalize Violet's offer. It just so happens that our number one candidate was out of the country and had called to say he would be happy to accept our offer! What do I do now?

I backpedaled to where we were before the call interrupted us and was literally thinking on my feet as I completed my sentence to Violet:

"And that's why I think the ... sales assistant position would be just right for you at this point in your career!"

What did I just do? While we did have this position open, she hadn't applied for it, it was more an administrative support position, and she was overqualified for it.

Violet later confided that she knew exactly what had happened because of the exasperated expression on my face when I took the call. This had become a bait-and-switch offer. So what did she do? Did she become offended? Did she let her ego get the best of her?

No. She accepted the position with a determination to prove me wrong. She maintained her positive attitude and brought a work ethic and drive for success that inspired countless others. She later shared with her colleagues that the sales assistant position proved to be just right for her because she was able to observe and learn from the positive and negative attributes of the other financial consultants and evolve on her own. And her success led us to realize the importance of hiring a higher quality individual for this entry-level position. We learned to appreciate the benefits of "growing your own" investment professional, and the sales assistant hiring process was more aggressive and impressive after that.

Violet ended up replacing our number one candidate within six months of employment. When she received her promotion, she publicly stated a goal of finding and investing $1 million per month. Most of our performance-oriented financial consultants were more than happy to inform her that this was not possible. "Not with this company, it can't be done!" they said.

These same consultants would belittle her optimism and challenge her investment expertise. Violet never presented herself as the smartest investment consultant, but she was able to connect with her clients on an emotional level and earn their trust, and then she would research suitable investment choices and products and confidently make her recommendation. Because these clients felt comfortable with her, oftentimes they would accept a more basic investment strategy. For them, making sure they didn't lose a lot of money became even more important than trying to make a lot of money. Sure, they could find someone with a more sophisticated investment proposition, but working with Violet was almost like working with their granddaughter.

Violet proceeded to set a new standard for performance, and she was named Rookie of the Year at our annual sales conference.

Her success and ability to inspire others to action was not limited to investment clients. I remember meeting a young lady who worked in another entry-level position in Violet's branch office, and she told me that Violet had inspired her to go back to school.

Because of Violet and the success of others to follow, our firm was now able to attract higher level, more experienced financial consultants. I was able to be more selective and recruit consultants who demonstrated more of a learning orientation, who found inspiration from being part of a team environment, and who enjoyed each other's company. The bar of success and personal income levels went way up at this "poor me, why am I here?" investment company. I even moved up the ladder and, within a few years, found myself leading seven managers and more than 100 financial consultants. The company and the people I had the opportunity to work with changed my life and provided me with numerous emotional and financial refining moments.

Over the years, Violet continued to grow and has now launched a sales training and speaking career that is providing inspiration to countless others.

So where does Violet's passion come from? What are some of the significant refining moments in her life? It turns out you have to go back a generation or two to fully appreciate the refining moments that have shaped her story.

Violet comes across as the product of an affluent Southern California way of life—self-assured, personable, physically attractive, and following a healthy lifestyle of diet and exercise. Because she was from Orange County, I teased her about basically having it all—growing up with the rich and famous, attending college in the beautiful city of San Francisco, dressing just right.

That's when she said to me, "If you only knew."

Violet is the child of Russian Jews. When she was young, her parents faced a significant refining moment: they determined to seek a better life for their family and decided to immigrate to the United States. Her father gave up everything they had, including a career, to move to America with nothing. He had to start all over again, with a language barrier and a menial job in Southern California. He pushed himself, and his family, very hard as he worked his way back up in the employment ranks to provide a nice middle-class lifestyle for them. The expectations and the level of discipline her father dished out certainly exceeded that of the other children in her neighborhood.

In elementary school, Violet felt like the awkward, out-of-place, ugly duckling. The other students teased her for her long curly-kinky hair, her lack of proficiency with the English language, and for being a "commie." Later in life, Violet's college sweetheart was killed in a motorcycle accident.

Violet's poise and achievement appeared to come so naturally and without effort. **Where did her strength and perseverance come from?**

Those are exactly the same questions she pondered when she observed her grandmother's strength, drive, determination, and joy. Violet would question these attributes in her grandmother, knowing the horrors her grandmother had experienced as a survivor of the Holocaust. She could have been bitter, but she wasn't; she faced the future with gratitude, hope, and expectation. Violet's financial success was a direct result of a history of emotional and physical triumph. Violet did in fact inherit her success, but her greatest inheritance had nothing to do with anything of monetary value.

Ten years later, the student becomes the teacher. I had an opportunity to sit in the back of a conference room as Violet gave a presentation to a group of financial professionals in Denver. She had been hired as an outside consultant, an expert on performance and motivation. From where I sat, I saw the participants' heads nodding in agreement. They were relaxed, laughing at her humor, enjoying the break from their daily routine. Violet was connecting with her audience. I, too, was listening and taking notes. It felt great—my former student was inspiring me!

CHAPTER 20

BANK TELLER TO CEO: "MR. WILSON"

YEARS AGO MY WIFE AND I had an opportunity to tour the United States Naval Academy in Annapolis, Maryland. This was not a public tour; we had boarded a military plane at the Los Alamitos Naval Base in Southern California and flew with others employed in the educational field for a project my wife was involved in. She and I have often flown together to some fine destinations as part of my business trips; this time, I was the guest spouse. The military plane was not even close to luxury travel, but it was by far our most impressive flight ever. I was humored when our military "flight attendant" in military fatigues came by with a cart and charged us for any and all snacks (of course, commercial airlines were soon to follow suit).

When we landed at Andrews Air Force Base, we were transported to the naval academy, where we would spend the next couple of days. We had an opportunity to interact with an impressive group of cadets in a variety of settings, including the classroom, dining hall, and a formal reception. I was so impressed by the experience that I became a mentor for the academy, basically an advocate for our local high school campuses.

Thousands of students apply to the academy each year, and only a small group are accepted. So imagine how someone would feel after being accepted into the academy only to later be rejected.

The year was 1976, and a member of a neighboring high school graduating class, a certain individual who I will refer to as Mr. Wilson, had applied to one of our nation's military service academies. The school was impressed with his academic performance and leadership qualities. The joy and exuberance he felt when he read his letter of acceptance must have been unmatched. This was an enormous refining moment.

The next refining moment, however, was just around the corner. It turns out 1976 was the year our nation's service academies were going to start adding female cadets into their ranks. The acceptance guidelines changed, Mr. Wilson no longer made the cut, and he received a second letter starting, "We regret to inform you …".

We regret to inform you …

While I can imagine that he took more than a few moments to wonder "why me?" there simply was no time to lose. He had to chart a new course of action. He enrolled in the state college and got a part-time job. That summer, instead of wearing impressive military dress blues, he was wearing a teller's name tag at the local bank. On the surface, it appeared to be a far cry from the opportunities afforded at one of the nation's most elite campuses.

So did this turn out to be a significant refining moment? We would have to ask Mr. Wilson from his office, where he is CEO of one of the nation's largest financial services organizations. He leads thousands of employees, interacts with U.S. presidents and CEOs across America, and is considered by many to be a financial services genius. But what impresses me the most is that he has maintained his small-town persona—he is a humble, lean and healthy, hardworking family man, someone who has embraced the ERM, PRM, and FRM moments in life.

I first met Mr. Wilson in the early 1990s, when he was a regional manager for a bank's consumer division in Southern California. Our two banks had merged. My mentor and manager, Joel, commented to my fellow district managers, "Wait until you meet Mr. Wilson. He is intelligent, driven, and highly personable. He is going to be a great business partner."

Joel was correct. There was something special about Mr. Wilson, and it is not just from the perspective of 20/20 hindsight. From our very first meeting, he instilled confidence. I sensed that he was going to do quite well in his career, and I knew others were rooting for him. Mr.

> **Through each and every promotion, he leveraged his daily refining moments.**

Wilson had worked his way up from part-time teller, and as a teller, and through each and every promotion, he leveraged his daily refining moments. I later discovered that he and I grew up in neighboring middle-class communities about 25 miles east of Los Angeles, and we'd graduated from rival high schools. I was saddened when Mr. Wilson eventually decided to follow one of his mentors to a banking group in the Midwest.

Fast-forward around 20 years, and I am considering a move to Denver to join the investment subsidiary of a major bank. As I conduct my due diligence on the corporation, who do I find is there? Mr. Wilson, president and considered to be next in line to assume the CEO position from his longtime mentor. When I had the opportunity to reconnect with him at a corporate event in southern Colorado, I walked up to introduce myself. Before I could say anything, Mr. Wilson warmly extended his hand, smiled, and said, "Hello, Greg." Others have said that Mr. Wilson had developed a memory like none other; I am confident this skill set is one of many he has that serve him well.

It is clear to me that Mr. Wilson learned to accept, create, and capitalize on the emotional, physical, and financial refining moments throughout his life. Part of his success has been that he surrounds himself with those who not only are intelligent but also have a strong desire for him to be successful.

The next time your bank teller or other service worker asks the question, "Can I help the next person in line?" pay attention and greet that person warmly. You could be meeting the future CEO of a major corporation.

You could be meeting the future CEO.

CHAPTER 21

SEASON OF TRANSITION

WHAT FOLLOWS IS ACTUALLY AN introduction to the next person's profile because of how his life wove into mine at a time of significant change for me and my family.

In 2006 we decided to move to the beautiful state of Colorado. We were lifelong Californians and three years earlier, I had been relocated from the southern half of the state to the northern half. Becky had assured me that once our sons were launched off on their own, she would have no objection to relocating. Our eldest son, Michael, had remained in Los Angeles; our middle son, Nick, was now working out of Portland, Oregon; and our youngest, Jon, informed us that he, his wife, Shon, and their twins, Luke and Paul, were moving to Denver. Our grandkids were not even a year old! Where was the refining moment here?

One afternoon, I was sitting in my home office when a former business colleague, John Sturgis, called me out of the blue. I hired John in the early '90s and he had been our firm's Rookie of the Year. We had reconnected by chance 20 years later, and now he was calling me with a question: "Hey, what do you think about Denver? One of our managers (of his present investment firm) is stepping down, and I thought about you."

I paused for a brief moment. My son's father-in-law had just given his notice (after being with the same company for 19 years) and now they would be moving to Colorado to be close to the grandchildren. I responded excitedly that yes, I was definitely interested!

To my surprise, Becky had no hesitation. After all, there were two grandkids in the equation.

It turns out that the hiring manager for the Denver position was based in northern California. At the interview, any concerns I had about joining a new firm were put to rest—Senior Vice President Chuck Shreve was a man of character and integrity. A refining moment! We would be moving to Denver!

I arrived in December 2005. Becky stayed behind to sell our home and joined me in April 2006. We settled on a home about an hour south of Denver, in a forested area at an elevation of around 6,700 feet. The deer roamed freely throughout our development, we had an occasional bear, fox, or mountain lion, and the panoramic views off the deck were breathtaking. When I sat on that deck, I would often reflect on how blessed we have been and how much distance we have traveled in our life journey. I think about the various people whose paths I have crossed and who have played a role up in my life to this point—business contacts, friends, associates, on and on. I have been blessed and am grateful, but life will continue to throw us a few curveballs, especially if we slip into a sense of complacency.

> **Life will continue to throw us a few curveballs.**

Becky and I had done it: we had raised our kids! Mission accomplished! But for a season, we were contemplating parting ways. It did not just happen overnight, and it certainly was not going to be resolved overnight. And yet, here we were, more than 30 years into our relationship, and we were going to have to invest some time and effort—again!—if we were going to stay together. I think a key issue for me was the foolish thinking that our mission was accomplished. In reality, our mission is never accomplished, and looking back, that season helped inspire me to inventory my thoughts over the years and start penning this book.

Becky and I had to redefine and refine our new lives, as individuals and as a couple, here in Colorado. I knew, from past experience, that I could not rely solely on my career and business associates for personal fulfillment.

Becky's refining moments led her to become a volunteer firefighter and emergency medical technician, a group that quickly became an extended family. I found myself joining a high-energy, contemporary band through a local community church. It had been several years since I had performed, but I was determined to dust off the keyboards and start practicing again.

We have since made countless lifelong friends in our neighborhood, work associations, and church. There are two musicians whose paths we have crossed who have become a significant and inspirational part of our lives: Dan and Kollette Decker. Dan plays the bass guitar, and Kollette has one of the most aggressive, beautiful voices I have ever come across.

I have selected Dan as my third and final profile as it seems we were going through some significant refining moments at about the same time. I have learned to open up and become more vulnerable with Dan, which, you must know, does not come naturally to us guys. My association with Dan and his friendship have proved to be a significant refining moment, and I would like for you to hear his story.

CHAPTER 22

RAGS TO RICHES TO CONTENTMENT: DANIEL DECKER

I'M CHOOSING TO TELL HIS story as an interview because it helps to hear it in his voice rather than mine.

Greg: Dan, I remember when I first met you. I was invited to check out the band and show up for a rehearsal at your home. I drive up past your gate, up the circular driveway to an impressive home. There is a motorhome bus, some ATVs, a boat—it was immediately apparent that you've enjoyed a fair amount of financial success. Jumping ahead for a bit, it wasn't until a couple of years later that I learned you had sold a business for a pretty nice sum of money.

Dan: Yes, that's right. My dad and another family business partner and I sold our business in 2004 for $10.5 million cash."

Greg: Based on some of the usual barometers that I tend to measure wealth (fine clothes, cocky arrogance, etc.), I had no idea for the first couple of years of our casual friendship that you were a multimillionaire. You must have come from a family of wealth and social stature, right?

> **It doesn't matter where you come from, what matters is where you are going.**

Dan: Ha! We were the kids referred to on the school bus as the Dirty Deckers. We were a bunch of hicks. We would literally get on the bus with straw in our hair from feeding the animals. We would head from Sedalia into Castle Rock with kids that looked way different than us. My first day home from junior high, I told my dad, "You're not cutting my hair anymore!"

Greg: It's apparent that you have grown past some of your childhood trauma, because it is obvious you have traveled a significant distance in terms of monetary wealth. But it turns out, as I was getting to know you much better and our friendship was growing, you were headed back down the financial ladder and you were experiencing some major life changes, or refining moments. In fact, I knew of your first wife, Jenny, but I never met her. Her illness had progressed and it was not long after we met that she passed away and now you were a single dad, raising your beautiful daughter, Rachel. Let's back up and hear more of your story as you literally went from rags to riches to what I consider to be a state of contentment.

Dan: Well, like I said, I was raised in Sedalia, Colorado. We were a low to middle income blue-collar family. I am the eldest of three brothers and have three sisters. My dad has always been a hard worker, and I'd say about 75 percent of the time, he ran his own business. He did anything and everything to make a living. He picked up his electronics training with his G.I. bill, he had a machine shop, he fixed TVs, drove trucks, had a trash-hauling business—basically anything to support his family. Our mom was a stay-at-home mother.

Greg: I know music is very important to you, and although you shy away from any compliments, you are a very talented musician—bass, banjo, guitar, and voice.

Dan: Yeah, music was always important to us. My dad and my uncle played country and bluegrass in local venues while we were growing up. At one point, they were the opening act for Tex Ritter at the Rocky Mountain Jamboree. Tex was so impressed with their music, he offered them an ongoing gig in California. It would have involved moving our family. That was a refining moment for my dad—you have to wonder how it would have worked out—but my dad declined because of our family.

Greg: So let's jump ahead to your business career. You have told me you did not attend college. How did you end up with such a successful business venture?

Dan: Well, I've actually had more failed businesses than ones that worked. For most of my working life, I have been self-employed. We were all trained as machinists, so we ran various machine shops and small businesses. My dad was just getting into RVing (recreational vehicles), and on his first trip he came close to being involved in a critical accident because he couldn't stop with the car he was towing.

> **I've actually had more failed businesses than ones that worked.**

In 1995, we had no large ambitions, but we started working on a supplementary braking system to help out my dad. I remember thinking, if this happened to my dad, it could probably happen to another 10, maybe 15 people. It turns out there was a great need for our product. We had substantial success, and we later sold the business to another company for $10.5 million.

Greg: So life was changing for you. I'm sure you experienced at least a few refining moments?

Dan: Yes and not always for the better. I remember pulling in around $50,000 to $60,000 per year from our braking business, more money than I had ever made. Then one day, my brother-in-law, our finance guy, calls me in and slips me a check across the desk. I look at it, and it is for $50,000! I asked him what it was for, and he said it was a bonus. I couldn't believe it! Soon, I started getting used to those checks. Before I knew it, my wife and I were living a dream I could have never imagined. Dinner with a big group? No problem, I'll pick up the tab.

Greg: I remember meeting you for breakfast once, at a regional airport here in Denver, and being shocked when you told me you used to charter those same beautiful jets parked outside the restaurant window. This was before I knew how much wealth you had accumulated. I was blown away. Again, I knew you had money, but you are this quiet, sometimes shy, reflective kind of guy. You are considerate and compassionate, and I know you would give the shirt off your back to help someone in need.

Dan: It was nothing for me to book a private jet, fly to Napa, and blow $30,000 on a vacation. That is how much my life had changed. Looking back, I am not always pleased with what I had become. I remember telling one of my employees, "You know, if you took all the money from the rich and gave it to the poor, it would all come back to the rich (me)." When we were negotiating the sale price of our business, the offer had already moved up a few times, and when they offered 10.5 mil, I snapped back, "I want $11 mil." I thought I was the best negotiator on the planet, when in reality I was this stupid cocky kid.

Greg: During this time of success, things weren't going so well on the home front.

Dan: My wife, Jenny, started getting sick. The business and my wife's health moved in opposite directions.

As the business was growing, her health was deteriorating. Our business was growing 200 to 300 percent per year, our revenues were over $13 million, and my wife was very sick. I would avoid or ignore the situation by going out and buying more toys, fancy clothes, swap out cars, just basically spend more money.

Greg: Dan, I know your faith is very important to you and a part of your daily life, but that was not the case back then, was it?

Dan: I grew up in church, but it meant nothing to me. In 2004 I sold our business and moved us into a big home. Jenny never even saw the entire property because she was so sick. Looking back, I can see where I completely isolated myself. I had no real friends. I had stopped attending any churches because my wife couldn't go. I even got to a point where my perception of women was at an all-time low. I felt emotionally and physically isolated from my wife because of her illness. I grew to a point where I feel I abandoned her emotionally and ignored her health. We had a big fight the night before she died. That was our last conversation.

Greg: There was probably some relief and guilt associated with your wife's death. Her suffering was finally over, but now you are a single dad. How did you cope or deal with your new situation?

Dan: Not very well at all. It was the end of 10 years of her illness. Our daughter, Rachel, was going through a lot of emotional and psychological distress. She would be off in a corner alone, and I would basically drink my-self to sleep.

Greg: You know my thoughts on Faith, Family, Friends, Fitness, and Finance. It sounds like you were bottoming out in at least the first four, and here comes the final: finance.

Dan: Absolutely. I was at the bottom, and the finances were just starting to crash right after Jenny died.

Greg: Up to this point, what were the best years of your life?

Dan: When we didn't have anything, and we lived in our small little house.

Greg: So what happened next?

Dan: A couple of things. Shortly before Jenny died, some friends from our past that really cared about me invited us to Plum Creek Community Church. It had been two years since I had stepped foot in a church. ... I started playing in the band and met some new people.

Greg: So this is the start of a refining process. Everything is great from here on out?

Dan: The start, yes, but there was a lot more to come. I sold my home in 2004 to move into a smaller house with Rachel and, fortunately, I sold just before the real estate bubble burst. I was investing around $20,000 per month into another business, and I kept selling stock to cover my expenses. My investment broker suggested opening up a credit line [margin account], so I could leave my investment portfolio intact. The plan was to cover the interest cost on the credit line with my investment earnings. It was working out great until the market started to drop. All of a sudden, I had to start selling stock and keep selling to cover my loan. In the end [March 2009], my $3 million portfolio turned into $400,000.

When I interviewed Dan for the first part of his story, Kollette was just about to enter his life. When she did, it became apparent to those of us who knew them best that they were being drawn to each other, almost as if their collective years of refinement had prepared them for these moments together. I fondly recall playing a song on the piano for their beautiful Colorado outdoor wedding!

Kollette was suddenly cast into the role of stepmother to a pre-teen daughter. But Dan and Kollette were in agreement that they wanted to add more children to their life as soon as possible. We were joyful when we learned of Kollette's pregnancy with twins, but from the very beginning it was characterized as a high-risk pregnancy. Still, Kollette was in excellent condition.

There was much reason for concern when Kollette, well into her final trimester, received a call from her physician informing her that she must rush to the hospital for additional testing. What followed was four weeks of hospitalization, a serious risk of life for Kollette, and, ultimately, the loss of their twins.

While Kollette and Dan grieved, I could not help but notice an awe-inspiring response of love and support from family and numerous close friends. Kollette's room was decorated with cards, posters, and well wishes, and they were surrounded with the thoughts and prayers of too many to count.

Are you fully investing in your refinement plan?

The situation that faced Dan, Kollette, and Rachel was one that would tap into the full resources of their "refinement plan." While they may not have thought in terms of refinement planning, think about it:

Financially: They had the financial means to access the best health care and cover the associated costs of being away from home.

Physically: Dan and Kollette led an active, healthy lifestyle. This was critically important for the level of stress they were experiencing and obviously contributed to Kollette's survival from associated complications during her recovery.

Emotionally/spiritually: They did not go it alone. All the money in the world could not have replaced the outpouring of emotional and spiritual support that they received.

Dan and Kollette were "fully invested" for a rainy day such as this.

Some time has passed since I interviewed Dan for this book. He and Kollette have added a beautiful son named Ladan to their family. Their relationship is even stronger, and they are more in love than when they first married.

Dan has launched, with the backing of some venture capital, yet another business with a highly improved modification of a previously successful product. This time, however, more than the backing of investors, Dan has the backing of a true support system: he is in constant communication with his God and his spouse. The couple continues to refine their lives together, and Rachel is a beautiful, socially adjusted young woman who has experienced much to this point in her young life and will continue to be refined toward her perfect purpose.

While I would not wish the hardship or challenges that Dan experienced on anyone, I cannot imagine knowing Dan any other way. He has been refined into the man I consider my friend. When I lost a job during the midst of the Great Recession, I could count on Dan to call or text me with words of encouragement. He would even tell me he was praying for me. What a perfect example of the kind of friend everyone needs in their corner. I was at a low point where I had no choice but to humbly accept his encouragement and prayers—no pretense, no male posturing. We had both experienced monetary wealth and setback, and we were both rebuilding our careers, but this time with a goal of contentment.

Will Dan's new business venture be just as successful—or, perhaps, even more successful than his wildest dreams? I certainly hope so. But that is not the point of this story. The goal for both of us is living and breathing our purpose with emotional, spiritual, physical, and financial contentment. I can guarantee you, we will both be aiming high.

CHAPTER 23

CLOSING THOUGHTS

WHEN A SON TAKES A part-time job at a local bank, could his hardworking dad have ever imagined that this would lead to a job as CEO of a major U.S. corporation?

When a young girl was struggling to survive in a concentration camp, could she possibly know that her strength and fortitude would breathe the inspiration of perseverance and success into her children and her children's children?

While a young father is performing at honky-tonks, did he know he was planting a gene of creativity in his inventor son that would grow into financial good fortune?

There are plenty of profiles about well-known successful people throughout history. But know this: there are no perfect people with perfect stories of success. I believe each of the individuals I profiled here feel called to an extraordinary purpose. I believe one skill set has set them apart from the masses: their ability to identify and capitalize on key opportunities or moments as they arise. If there is a door that appears to open, they walk through it. They have all experienced victories and setbacks, trials and triumphs, and they will all readily admit, like my grandfather did on his deathbed, "I have so much more room to grow."

The three individuals profiled here, and countless others whose path I have crossed, represent for me success with significance:
- Emotional wealth
- Physical wealth
- Financial wealth
- Living life to its fullest calling, purpose, and potential

Perhaps you found some similarities within these profiles to your own life's journey. Maybe some public figure or persons within your inner circle come to mind who, for you, exemplify an accomplished balance of ERM, PRM, and FRM. The more intentional you are in assessing the strengths of others, in each key area, the more deliberate you will become in developing your personally refining moments. True success is all around us, and, as the saying goes, success breeds success.

What is your story?

Give some thought to your personal profile. Write out your own profile as if you were going to be included in a future edition of this book. What is your story? As long as we are still occupying space on this good green earth, we are not a failure. We can turn any setbacks, lack of judgment, or shortcomings in our emotional, physical, and financial world into the next story of success. We can make a vow to travel an even greater distance today, tomorrow, and year after year.

Your circumstances do not define you, they refine you.

SECTION VI

REFINEMENT VS. RETIREMENT

(Which you probably can't afford anyway)

CHAPTER 24

YOUR FUTURE

SO WHAT DO I WANT to be when I grow up? What do your children want to be when they grow up? More importantly, what do YOU want to be when you grow up?

When my son Michael was finishing junior high school, I had one of those father-son conversations with him. "So, Son, you're getting ready to move on to high school. You have done really well in junior high, you are well liked, you are good in sports. It's probably time to start thinking about what you would like to do in the future. Any idea of what you want to be when you grow up?"

What do YOU want to be when you grow up?

To which my son replied, "I'm not sure, Dad." Long pause. "All I know is I want a job where if my son has a baseball game or I want to coach, I can be there."

Ouch. It looks like my son was already in the business of handing out refining moments!

As I look back, there was another refining moment that at the time seemed somewhat inconsequential, but, of course, there is no such thing. While I was vice president of future markets with Bank of America, I attended a direct marketing workshop in New York for insights on how to target the senior-mature population. I learned about changes in our attitudes and defining what is important to us as we age.

Our class was shown a video of a recent focus group meeting with a group of elderly people. I was in my mid-thirties at that time, and I was fascinated to observe these "old" people talking about "older" people, as if they were young and old age was somewhere off in their future. I thought *they* were the target audience of these focus group meetings?

It turns out our personal definition of "older" is usually 10 years beyond our own age. So, if a senior age 65 in this focus group is being asked questions about the older population, she or he is automatically thinking about someone who is at least 75 years of age.

When I was in my twenties, I figured I would be grown up at around age 35. Now that I am in my fifties, I think that certainly I will have my act together by the time I'm

65. Think about your past and present. Do you consider yourself a grown-up or old? At what age do you think you will have your act together and be oh-so-mature? Add 10 years to your current age and think about what you will look like physically, financially, and emotionally. What does life look like in general? What will you be doing for work and fun? What will be important to you?

Can anyone honestly say what they want to be when they grow up?

I don't think so. And that is the point. You are deceiving yourself if you think that someday, maybe in another 10 years, you will have your act together—greater financial security, better health, and better relationships. If I had waited until I had it "all together," I would never have penned this book. So rather than waiting to grow up, or living each day from a perspective of doubt, or beating myself up because I haven't arrived yet, I am going to give life a 100 percent effort at creating, observing, and learning from my daily refining moments. So as of this writing, I am a grown-up! And tomorrow, I will grow up even more.

Every single day, I can do something positive. By positive, I mean create forward motion in each of the three primary refinement categories that will in turn keep me on track with my overall life purpose.

You might be thinking, that while this sounds like a good idea and there are some interesting concepts here,

"You don't know what my life is like. As soon as things settle down, I will get around to at least a few of them."

We all have hectic days, and my intent to spend an hour or so at the gym just might not happen; but even with a busy travel day, I can purposefully consider and take action in each of the three broad refinement categories. Consider the following:

FRM: I am working today (making money), and I will park in the airport economy lot and skip the overpriced magazine counters (saving money).

PRM: I will walk at a faster pace from the parking lot to the ticket counter and through the airport; I will perform some basic stretches while waiting for the plane; and I will finish my day with squats, calf raises, sit-ups, and push-ups in my hotel room.

ERM: I will call my spouse at least twice today, drop a "thinking of you" e-mail to my kids, smile at everyone I come into contact with, hunt for an opportunity to provide assistance to someone in need during my workday, and end my day with a beneficial reading and a prayer of gratitude.

Now, I could approach the day with an "I deserve" and "tomorrow" attitude. I deserve to park in the high-cost lot, take the escalators, and spend 20 bucks on a shoe shine, snacks, and magazines before I board the plane. I will display that "look at me, I am an important businessman" smug expression throughout my day, and later drift off to sleep watching mindless television following my in-room cuisine of beer, cheeseburger, and fries. Tomorrow I will get back on track.

Been there, done that!

If we give conscious thought to and put effort into our daily refining moments, then we are living at 100 percent. As we continue with these patterns of thought and action, the conscious effort continues to foster and develop our unconscious mind, and we find ourselves living out our purpose in life.

This is just one simple illustration of what can be accomplished during what would otherwise feel like a hectic, out-of-control travel day. Obviously, with thoughtful planning and the investment of more time and energy, a more momentous approach would be to specifically target your greatest area of weakness:

If FRM is your greatest need: seek out a certified financial planner for debt reduction and the implementation of a disciplined savings and investment strategy.

If PRM is your greatest need: complete suggested medical evaluations based on your age and solicit the support of a certified personal trainer.

If ERM is your greatest need: take steps to reconcile your relationships and spiritual health with the assistance of a counselor, clergy, and/or spiritual advisor.

Even if you cannot afford professional assistance in your personal area of greatest need (an argument can be made that you cannot afford not to), there are numerous online resources and books available that, with deliberate effort, can greatly assist you in strengthening all three areas of growth. You might simply reach out to family, friends, or associates who have experienced greater success in your area of needed refinement.

If you are younger, or busy with career or family, this approach to living each day will make a difference in your life. If you are older and nearing or past the traditional age of retirement, you do not have to wait any longer to figure out what you want to be when you grow up; this approach to daily living will positively impact your life.

Does this really matter?

Yes. Because for everyone, there is a major demographic change under way that is greatly impacting and redefining our American way of life. That is: there is no gold watch.

CHAPTER 25

WHERE DO WE GO FROM HERE?

FOR THE MAJORITY OF AMERICANS, a traditional retirement will be absolutely unattainable. The ability to live in a manner in which you are accustomed while being supported by Social Security and income from your 401(k) and other investments will prove to be insufficient. This is a fact that is increasingly coming to light.

The very nature and concept of retirement is changing. The impact will be felt in our homes, in the workplace, in our educational and religious institutions, and the political environment for years to come.

We can lower our expectations or increase the number of our working years, or both. If you and I plan to be around for a long time (age 90 is the new 75), then we must truly embrace the human experience.

For me, the human experience includes the following:
- We need to love and be loved.
- People will disappoint you, loved ones will disappoint you, and you will disappoint you.
- Good things happen to "good" people and to "bad" people; and bad things happen to "bad" people and to "good" people.
- You will harvest what you plant.

I firmly believe the more goodness we plant, in our minds and in our actions, the more goodness we will receive. But understand that I am not proposing a feel-good, positive-thinking-only approach toward life. I'll let you in on a little secret: a life of continuous improvement, success, and significance involves both intellect and purposeful effort. We need to learn, and we need to work.

We cannot just think something into being. We need to develop, train, nurture, and expand our intellectual capacity. We then need to appropriate our intellectual capacity into action. You may do a fair amount of research, reading, training, and continuing education when it comes to your profession, but do you honestly put forth the same amount of effort and training into your health or developing better relationships? How many hours of continuing education did you invest in your marriage or children this past year?

A positive attitude is vitally important. But let's face it, not everything in life goes as planned, and that is part of the human experience. While you are planting your seeds of goodness, they may be falling on thorny, dry, desolate ground. The environment at home or in your workplace may not be as fertile or conducive to accepting these seeds of goodness.

There have been various catalysts for creating positive refining moments presented throughout this book, and if they are implemented, they will make your situation better. Don't worry if the circumstances around you seem to compete with your desire to live a life of continuous improvement. You can start today by taking daily steps in the right direction, as these catalysts or positive actions from an emotional, physical, and financial perspective all start with you.

> **You can start today by taking daily steps in the right direction.**

Life in general will not always go as planned. You can raise three children in the same home, and they can each grow to approach life from a different perspective. You can do well in school, pick up a lucrative degree, marry at a desired age, and have 2.5 children, yet fall far short of what you had thought you would accomplish up to this point in your life.

Not every interaction or involvement with others will go as planned or as desired. Most people I come into contact with seem to be positive individuals, and I value my association with them. Quite frankly, there are some people who rub me the wrong way—our values are totally different, and their temperament brings me down.

But guess what? More than likely, they feel the same way about me! Years ago, I heard a minister share that when someone rubs you the wrong way, think in terms of "heavenly sandpaper": maybe that person was meant to smooth off some of your rough edges. Yet another definition of refinement.

The human experience for me is to learn from every experience, every situation, and everyone I come into contact with. The human experience involves paying it forward from a personal lifelong learning perspective. You might in fact be just the right person to assist someone going through an extremely challenging situation that you have personally survived.

What has your life uniquely qualified you for? How to survive or repair a broken relationship? How to deal with the unexpected loss of a job? How to love others unconditionally? How to turn your life around from a physical setback? How to keep moving forward when common sense says to stop, give up, and retreat?

Look around you. There are countless opportunities to serve others while you selfishly or selflessly invest in your emotional and spiritual well-being. What do I mean by selfishly? Talk to someone volunteering in a homeless shelter food line. Talk to someone helping out with the children or teenagers at their local church. Talk to the elderly volunteer who stopped by my hospital room with a visitation dog just to brighten my day. All of these people bring joy and are of a direct benefit to others, but they will be the first to admit, perhaps even with a little embarrassment, that serving others brings even greater joy and enrichment to their own life.

Again, why does all of this matter? Our entire economy is adapting to substantial changes with the aging population and shifting demographics. I am certain we will see numerous changes in our lifetime partially driven by the sheer number of baby boomers transitioning into their senior phase of life. Many "seniors" will start new businesses, invent new products, discover a new hobby, join a theater group, or start a rock band. They will provide meaningful contributions to society as a whole while fully living in their "golden" years.

Serving others brings even greater joy and enrichment.

From a practical perspective, many seniors will need to seek the emotional and financial support of extended families or friends. For example, we will see more homes being built for extended households. These homes will have two master bedrooms, one of which is designed with greater ease and accessibility for the aging individual.

And you know what? I do not think any of this is necessarily a bad thing. With our continued modernization, mobilization, and perceived affluence, we have grown apart from family and friends. Text messages and e-mails are very convenient, but my fear is we are losing face-to-face contact and the sharing of our irreplaceable personality. So if economic uncertainty brings us back a few notches, so be it!

If, as I predict, we are being driven back toward each other, then let us play our A-game, be 100 percent all-in with this human experience, and forever develop and refine our emotional, physical, and financial well-being. Let's make sure that you like you, that your family has a desire to be with you, and that you have a significant network of friends and associates, because you may just be around for many years to come.

The majority of my professional career has revolved around the business of financial success and the attainment of a financially secure retirement. What I have learned over the years is that financial success without physical and emotional prosperity comes in at two-thirds short of your full potential. Who among us would want the following epitaph on their tombstone: "He lived life to one-third of its fullest"?

Furthermore, if you cannot fully fund a traditional retirement, then go into overdrive with developing your emotional and physical prosperity. Devote time and energy in your health, your appearance, your relationships, and your emotional and spiritual well-being. Forget retirement, which you may have determined you cannot afford anyway. Work and contribute just as long as you can, waking up each day cognizant of the fact that you are on a lifelong path of refinement, not retirement.

If you are younger than the traditional age of retirement, then recognize that the world around you has numerous refining moments waiting to be discovered. These refining moments will lead you toward a path of financial, physical, and emotional wealth, prosperity.

By loving others, being lovable, learning, and sharing with others your lessons learned, you will have lived a journey of success with significance.

By loving others, being lovable, learning, and sharing with others your lessons learned, you will have lived a journey of success with significance. So do not waste any time:

- Do your homework, continuously evaluate your progress, and invest wisely, every single day, into the financial, the physical, and the emotional bank of the human experience.
- Forget retirement. Continue to share your refining moments and continue to learn from the moments of others.
- Associate with like-minded individuals, and gently reach out and lead others you come into contact with who can use some assistance in discovering their own purpose in life.

As of today, your awareness level is way up, and you cannot help but notice the financial, physical, and emotional refining moments that each day has to offer. My hope for you is that you will fully appreciate and find tremendous fulfillment in developing these moments as you live out your life's purpose.

MEET THE AUTHOR

GREG HERNANDEZ WENT FROM BEING a fast-food worker to a respiratory therapist and then entered the financial planning world at the age of 27. Throughout his career, he worked for major corporations including Bank of America and Merrill Lynch, enjoying prosperous times before having to practically start over, more than once during his 28-year career.

But starting from scratch meant having to come to an understanding of the factors that landed him in all of his positions, good and bad. He learned to identify, embrace, and implement improvement opportunities at critical moments along the way—known as refining moments.

In 2013, Greg's passion for living a life of continuous improvement and inspiring others to higher levels of success and significance led him to launch his own speaking, training, and consulting practice. For more information, or to have Greg speak to your audience, visit www.GKarlCo.com.

www.ingramcontent.com/pod-product-compliance
Lightning Source LLC
Chambersburg PA
CBHW051752040426
42446CB00007B/334